Barbara S

# Secret of Santiago

# Secret of Santiago

## A Novel of Medieval Spain

Bernard Reilly

COMBINED BOOKS
*Pennsylvania*

## PUBLISHER'S NOTE

Combined Books, Inc., is dedicated to publishing books of distinction in history and military history. We are proud of the quality of writing and the quantity of information found in our books. Our books are manufactured with style and durability and are printed on acid-free paper. We like to think of our books as soldiers; not infantry grunts, but well dressed and well equipped avant garde. Our logo reflects our commitment to the modern and yet historic art of bookmaking.

We would like to hear from our readers and invite you to write to us at our offices in Pennsylvania with your reactions, queries, comments, even complaints. All of your correspondence will be answered directly by a member of the Editorial Board or by the author.

We encourage all of our readers to purchase our books from their local booksellers, and we hope that you let us know of booksellers in your area that might be interested in carrying our books. If you are unable to find a book in your area, please write to us.

For information, address:
COMBINED BOOKS, INC.
1024 Fayette Street
P.O. Box 307
Conshohocken, PA 19428



Map by Lizbeth Nauta.

*Library of Congress Cataloging-in-Publication Data*
Reilly, Bernard F., 1925-
Secret of Santiago : a novel of medieval Spain/Bernard Reilly.
p. cm.
ISBN 0-938289-60-8
1. Spain—History—Fiction.
2. Santiago de Compostela (Spain)—Church history—Fiction.
3. Civilizaiton, Medieval—Fiction. I. Title.
PS3568.E4845T738 1996
813'.54—dc20 96-32516
CIP

Combined Books Edition 1 2 3 4 5

First published in the USA in 1997 by Combined Books, Inc.

First Edition, First Printing 1997
Printed in the United States of America.

*To Marge then...*

*To Marge now*

# Chronology

| | |
|---|---|
| A.D. 711-713 | Muslim conquest of Visigothic Spain |
| A.D. 719 | Victory of Pelayo at Covadonga |
| A.D. 731 | Venerable Bede publishes *Ecclesiastical History* |
| A.D. 732 | Charles Martel repulses Muslim invasion of France |
| A.D. 791 | Beginning of the reign of Alfonso II |
| A.D. 798 | Alfonso II's sack of Muslim Lisbon |
| A.D. 800 | Charlemagne crowned Holy Roman Emperor |
| A.D. 800? | Alfonso II creates the bishopric of Oviedo |
| A.D. 830 | Bishop Teodemir of Iria Flavia discovers the relics of Saint James the Great |
| A.D. 830? | Alfonso II authorizes the building of the first shrine-church at Santiago de Compostela |
| A.D. 842 | Death of Alfonso II, king of Asturias |
| A.D. 878 | Alfred defeats Danes at Edington |

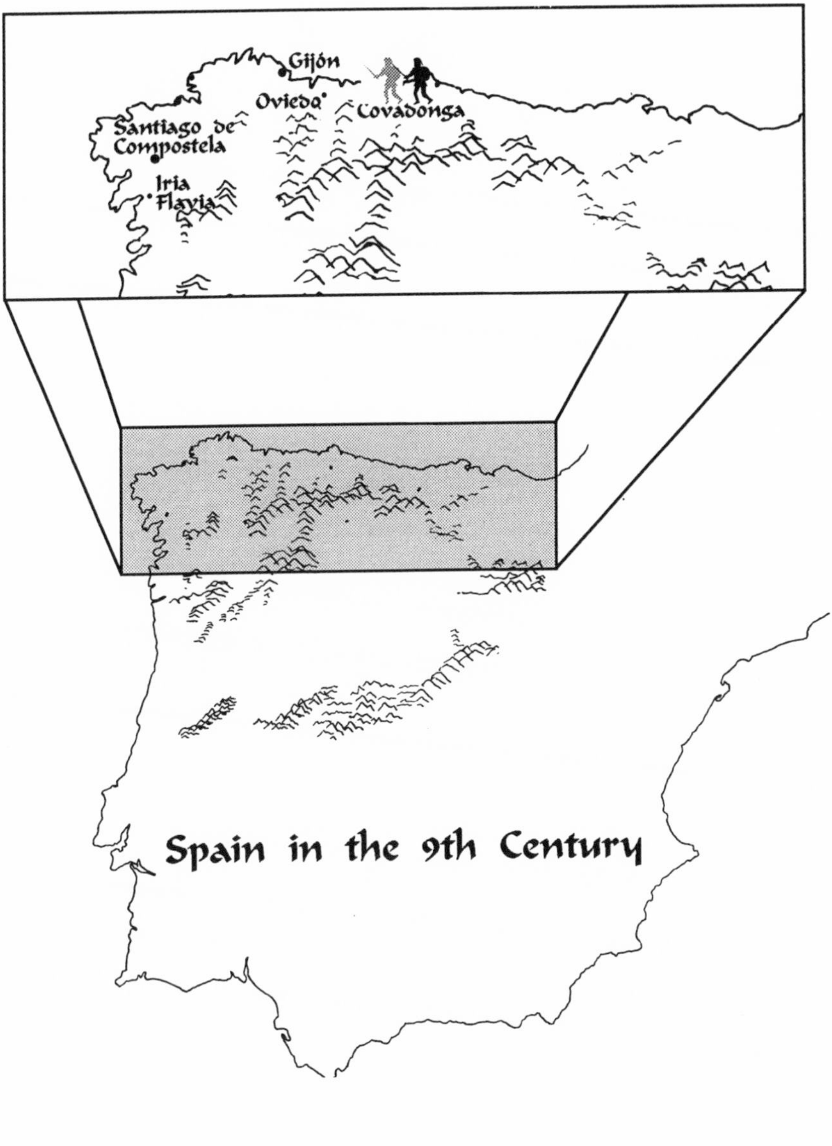
Gijón
Oviedo
Covadonga
Santiago de Compostela
Iria Flavia
Spain in the 9th Century

# Secret of Santiago

# Chapter One

The deer was right down there. Just off the path. Under the fur-brown hide the muscles would be tensed, bunched, ready to explode into a blur of motion and grace. Head erect, he would be testing the air, casting back and forth for the scent that spelled danger. Just off the path and half-hidden by the blend of shade and late-morning sun. But he was there.

In the split second after Oro had glimpsed him and gone to earth, the buck had sensed something—someone. But now the hunter was himself in cover. Motionless, head pressed close against the earth, his dark hair might itself have been some groundcover, blackened by the winter hardly over, where it thrust forward from the brush at the top of the rise. It was a test of patience now. If he could be still long enough, the deer would uncoil, would resume feeding on the new shoots of sapling about it. Then he could ease back, angle to the right below the ridgeline, and come up from its rear for a shoulder shot. He was upwind. The animal could not smell him. Unless he was careless, snapped a branch or kicked a stone, it would not hear him. But until it took up grazing again, it was too dangerous even to begin to ease himself back. Those great, liquid eyes would catch the slightest motion, the legs would flex, and it would be lost into the forest before he himself had scuttled back an inch.

"Aaaaugh!" The breath went out of him in one great, thunderous exhalation. His face thrust forward into the dirt and moss. His ribs bent against the rock and forest cover beneath him. He lost his grip on his bow and his quiver leapt down and forward against his neck and right ear. Even before the pain came, before his mind could register it, he knew that the deer was lost.

"Caught, Oro, caught! The hunter hunted, taken! I took you and you never had a clue!"

The soft, fleshy weight grinding him into the forest floor had a name. It was Neppy. That idiot. That fat fool. His breath still came in gasps. His anger built as his surprise faded but his shocked limbs would not do his bidding. The weight of the other still pinned him, still humiliated him as he thrashed under it, trying ineffectively to throw it off.Then he was free. Neppy had rolled off of him, half-laughing, half-giggling in the way he had. Laying there in the forest brush beside him.

"Christ, Oro, you look like a gut-shot deer yourself. Rolling around. Trying to get your wind back. Scrabbling in the dirt, you are. Imagine that. Your lovely cousin a mighty hunter and you the prize."

Oro tried to hook him then. Rolling over he jerked his left knee up, trying for Neppy's groin. But his muscles failed him. They were still half in shock. Anyway the fat of the other's thighs protected him, would probably have deflected the knee even if he'd had the strength to speed it properly.

"Come on, Oro, it was a joke. It was a game. I just wanted to see if I could do it. I didn't want to hurt you—but I could have if I had wanted to!"

Both boys were scrambling to their feet now. The heavy

one, Nepotian, brushing his bulk, tugging his clothes into place, half-smiling and half-anxious now as he regarded his taller cousin. He knew that he had gone very far indeed. His crazy, sly humor, his never more than half-hidden jealousy and sometimes even dislike of Oro, had betrayed him into foolishness again. He felt like the fool! He was flushed, embarrassed, and a little apprehensive.

Aurelius could feel the blood pounding in his temples. His limbs trembled even as the strength began to pour back into them. His bow lay disregarded at his feet but his knife, never lost to the shock ot their collision, was out, clear of its leather scabbard. Crouching slightly he began to advance on the other, sliding each foot forward in turn, feeling the ground through his moccasins, the point of the knife ever advancing towards the fat one's belly. His target gave ground. Drew his own knife now. But the older boy, the heavier boy, wanted no fight. Still, he could not turn and run. But backing up like this he might trip and his nutty cousin would be on him.

"Wait a minute, Oro. I didn't mean to make you crazy mad. It was just—well, you know—like the Ram always says. When you're hunting you always have to be conscious of the forest watching you. You can't ever let your prey take up your whole attention or you'll never catch it. But that's just what you were doing. That's why I could surprise you. I thought that I should show you that. Teach you a little, maybe. But I guess I went too far, huh?"

"Too far! You great lump of shit! That was going to be my first deer and then you came along with your silly games. Now I'll teach you a lesson. Now I'm going to carve up a little of that fat hide of yours. See how funny you think it is when you bleed, you great bucket of guts."

The slim, raven-haired boy moved yet again towards his

cousin, pressing him, maneuvering him, never allowing him time to cast a glance behind and pick a line of retreat. Now he had him. Neppy had backed up against a mature oak. Oro was too close for him to sidle off one way or the other. The fat boy chose. Raising his left arm half above his head, he cast his own knife lightly at the feet of his cousin.

"I won't fight you, Oro. I can't fight you. And you can't fight me. You know that. You know what our uncle would say. You know that he has forbidden anyone to fight us, or to harm us in any way. He won't let us fight one another—at least to the point of drawing blood. What do you think he'll do to us if you stab me? Do you think that he's going to forgive either one of us? Do you think that he'll take you for any less crazy than me? Or maybe more?"

The knifepoint was at his belly. Nepotian was sweating in great rivulets. But he held his eyes steady on those of his cousin. And the knife stopped. It didn't go away but it didn't press into his flesh either.

"And think of the Ram," he blurted. "Think about how he'll use this. Our uncle favors him a little already because he's the oldest. Give him the chance and he'll build on that. Play the mature warrior. Play the almost heir, the almost king! He'll understand us to death. Go on about having to remember that we're really young. And the more that he excuses us the more that he pushes himself to the front. Do you want to lose our chance—your chance—before you even have it?"

Oro knew that he was not going to kill him. He knew that he never would have. Now he could not bring himself even to draw a little blood. But Neppy could not be sure of that and it was sweet revenge to see—to hear him whine. Gradually he closed on his cousin, ran the knife ever so gently up his chest to just below his Adam's apple. The other ceased to speak, not convinced that his former victim did not intend to cut him. Kill him? While Neppy's attention was riveted on the knifepoint Oro brought up his knee and began to grind it lightly into the other's groin. He pressed it into the fat held motionless by the oak.

Still Nepotian did not move or speak. He did go very white and his throat bobbed trying to control a growing nausea. The pain was not unbearable but it threatened to become terrible at any second. Then it stopped, Oro took his knee away, and he was free to slide down against the tree bark. He cradled his knees in his arms and waited for the pain to subside.

"You are an idiot. Do you know that, Nepotian? Some one is going to kill you someday. Not me. Maybe the Ram. Maybe Ramiro. I'm trying to get the first deer of my life. Everyone has to get their first or nobody ever takes them for a man. And you have to skulk along behind me waiting for a chance to do something idiotic. For a kid's game you ruin the hopes of five hours' hunting."

"Would you be surprised if I killed you? What in the hell did you expect me to do? Was I supposed to chase you and throw branches and leaves at you like we did when we were kids?"

Aurelius stopped because he could feel his own anger rising again. His own words chafed and bruised his own bitterness. God, how he hated being taken always for a kid. He had fifteen years. He was a man's age. He was too old for these stupid games.

"Come on, Oro. Don't be so grim. You'll get your deer. Everyone does sooner or later. Even I got mine."

It was true, Nepotian thought with some surprise. I'm a good shot even though I don't like blundering about in the cold and the rain of the woods. People don't expect a fat boy to be good at anything much but they know that I can outshoot most of them, the great, gross ignoramuses.

"If it comes to that, Ramiro himself will take you out and see that you get your deer. Honor of the family, you know?"

That had been a mistake, to say that. Christ, but Oro was touchy. He wanted so badly to be the complete warrior. He couldn't wait to be blooded. Nobody could help him. No one but me can even talk to him this spring.

"Forget it, Oro, forget it! There's more than one way to be a man. How about if we go down by the river. The women will be washing there. They're always sure that some of the men are watching them from the trees while they wash. They'll be splashing one another, tickling one another, hiking up one another's skirts—to tease their audience. Why should all that go to waste? Let's go down there and take a peek. It'll stir up your loins. Make you feel like the man you are."

Aurelius looked at his cousin, exasperated and maybe a bit amused now.

"A minute ago you were playing child's pranks, then you were going on about being kingly. Now you want to go steal glimpses of washer-women's behinds. Are you ever really serious, Neppy, or is it all one big joke to you?"

Nepotian knew that he had his audience now. Oro was so serious. It was his favorite word. But he could be amused too. Nepotian knew how to work him from a thousand boyhood confidences. How often had they rolled on the ground, weak with laughter? And who supplied the joke? Oro could see the ridiculous side but he couldn't invent it. That took a mind like his own.

"Sex is serious, Oro. It's even kingly. Remember what Pelayo said about hairballs? Put the balls to the hair and a new people is born! It could be our royal duty. Not a bad duty either, do you think?"

"What I think is that our uncle would take an oak switch to your shoulders and maybe more. You think that he would be angry if I had put a hole or two in your fat hide. How would he like it if someone caught his loving nephews lying on their bellies and spying on the women? Goats in rut! And what would the Ram make of that. Not just childishness, he would say, but vicious perversity. Small-minded, immature curiosity. Sinful. Scarcely regal."

"Our uncle's problem is our uncle's problem, Oro. Everbody does it. It keeps up our numbers. Anyway, I won't carry tales about you and you won't tell them about me. As for Ramiro, don't worry about him. He won't carry this sort of tale. He's lain between too many women's legs himself. If I wanted to, I could fill old uncle's head with a lot of stories of that kind about the Ram. And our cousin knows it."

Oro looked at his cousin. Nepotian was born with a sly look, he guessed. The red, curly hair, the pale blue eyes, the full face always mobile, never quite focusing fully on you. Fighting was not his way as it was cousin Ramiro's. But one could not be sure that his little intrigues were entirely serious either. He liked to tease. He liked to puzzle you. But he could be mean—he could delight in hurting you in small ways. Ramiro held him in contempt but was careful to avoid him as much as possible too.

"Well, are we going? Come on, Oro, come on. Maybe we can even get one of the girls to go to the woods with us. Think about that. Lose your virginity! You never have had one! I might get one for you. Instead of a deer in rut, a woman in rut! There's more than one forest sport if you're not too dull to see it."

The prospect was exciting but Aurelius knew that he could not be comfortable with his cousin in those circumstances, even if such a crazy thing really happened. They had shared a lot but this was different. And one could not trust him entirely. Neppy was always thinking. He was always thinking about a way to show himself off and he could get very careless when he tried to do that. At least, careless about other people's secrets.

"No. You run off to the river and get yourself all lathered up. Get yourself so hard that you ache. That's about all that you'll get. I'm going to see if I can find any other game to hunt. That is, if you haven't scared off everything this side of the mountains."

Aurelius walked off down the trail. His cousin watched him go with an expression that was, perhaps, a little sad. Soon enough it turned into something very like a pout.

# Chapter Two

The shadows swelled and sank. The bursting of resin, the crumbling of logs, the movement of people, all varied the long shadows that the flames cast on the new stone of the walls. The palace that Alfonso had built for his new royal city of Oviedo was still the marvel of his people.

Ramiro loved its display, its fresh grandeur. Of course, some of the old ones still grumbled that Oviedo was too exposed a site. They said that its fresh houses and new churches would see Muslim torches yet. The place was too short a march from the great pass over the mountains. Everyone knew that route; goatherds, bandits, Muslim slavers, traders. Guides wouldn't be hard to come by and a strong force could sweep out of the pass and be on the town before a decent alarm could rally its defenders.

Still, he thought, the ancient ones had probably said that about the move out of Cangis de Onis in the old days. They always did. If they were served out of a new winecup they asked what had been wrong with the old one. If a new privy was dug they complained because it was a few steps farther than the full one that they had used till then. Pity they didn't fall in and drown. Complain. Cough. Spit. Scratch themselves. What else did they ever do?

The young cousins had little but contempt for the elders,

the enemies of their uncle. They sat now, Ramiro, Nepotian, Aurelius, on a bench below his throne. They were raised above the rest and were going to have a great view of the bard. The Easter feasting was coming to a close with this celebration. All of the young men were just a little giddy with the wine they'd had but Ramiro was trying hardest to behave soberly. He sat very erect and still and both Aurelius and Nepotian thought that he looked wooden, like a church statue, rather than sober. Giggling at the idea, one or the other of them leaned against Ramiro from time to time to see if they could topple him. He was furious but of course could do nothing there under their uncle's eyes.

I'll fix them, he thought. Wait til tomorrow. God, I wish I hadn't drunk so much wine. I'm not sure I can keep it down. The hall is so hot with the mass and the stink of bodies. I'm queasy and these two fools keep shoving me. If I could just hold still and let my stomach settle. Fortunately for Ramiro, just then his tormentors were distracted.

A sudden skirl of pipes cut through the din of the great hall as the tale-teller took up his stance in the circle kept clear before the throne of Alfonso. Those who could find room to do so made themselves comfortable. They knew that the story to come would be long, suitably embellished, richly declaimed. The bard had a just fame and the occasion dictated his subject. He settled his goatskin pipes on the floor now, leaving his arms free to inscribe his pictures on the air.

"The time of the great raids had ended. The lean years were upon them. The Africans had pushed north beyond the mountains themselves. They had a great garrison and a governor at Gijón. When Pelayo or his band ventured out of the valley of Cangis de Onis they were always scouted. Small groups were cut off and down. Prisoners were sold into slavery. Some were crucified. The captains grumbled, the warriors deserted, the tribes melted into the hills."

This was what the audience expected. They knew the tale as well as the bard himself but he chanted it. He could bring it alive. He could warm their dreams.

"Now the great African emir, their chief in Córdoba, had sent reinforcements to Gijón. Young warriors for a spring campaign if the need be. He'd sent a new governor too. Musa he called himself. Young and anxious to make a great name, he called himself after the original conqueror of this land. He had the warriors needed to sweep the valleys with fire and sword as the spring opened them up—to kill the oxen, goats and sheep—to burn the huts -to murder the old and brain the newborn—to drive the men south in long queues to the slavemarkets of Córdoba and eventually perhaps the women after them. But first he had to talk. First he had to try to persuade the famous bandit, Pelayo, to surrender himself. That would be the real coup. To have that sacker of cities and slayer of governors come in like a lamb. Even at the head of his warband still. Let him lead them south to the service of the emir himself. With a strong escort, of course. Then everyone in the peninsula would have to concede the ability, the talents, of Musa.

"And so, the talks began. The African, Musa, the chief of the Astures, Bodo, and the great Goth, Pelayo himself. The weather was still too cold for fighting that spring. No time to lead troops into the field. So it was time to talk with your enemy. Time to take his measure. Time to study his resolve.

"But another one was watching as well. Amalsuntha. Pelayo's sister, Bodo's wife was fresh from her latest delivery. The strength had returned to her long, blond hair. The swelling had left her ankles. The muscles of her abdomen were reasserting their dominion. Her beauty was unimpaired. And she watched Musa. She watched to see if he in turn watched her and, when he did, she knew that her old power with men could still be trusted. Amalsuntha formed no great opinion of the young African but he would do. He was young. He was vain. He could be led by the nose—or somewhat lower on—as most men could. It was her time!"

A murmur ran through the audience. The bard heard it without appearing to have. Amalsuntha, the beautiful devil! They all knew the story of her enforced marriage to the chief of the Astures. They all knew that she had sworn revenge on her brother. They knew also that she despised the Astures as greasy hill bandits, unworthy of her station and her splendid favors, and her own husband she loathed most of all. The story of his murder had been told and retold and yet they envied him. Half of them out there would be feeling a stirring in their loins even as they thought of her. The young men especially.

"Bodo died in the night. He died in his own bed by the hand of his own wife as he slept the dreamless sleep of the satiate. His own knife sliced though the artery of his neck and he died before he could fully awake and without a sound. The old ones said that Amalsuntha took his private parts with her as well; for a gift and a surety of her intentions to her new ally, Musa. The night covered her and her old servant as she went to him in Gijón. Her three children by Bodo she left to be murdered by her hated relatives among the Astures. They were not her concern.

"In the fortress of the Africans at Gijón she brewed her evil. As she had foreseen, Musa received her with open arms. At table and abed, she became his tutor. The more her spell increased, the more he trusted her when she told him which of the chiefs of the Astures should be approached. She knew which had never approved of Bodo's alliance with the hated Visigoths and their chief. She knew who had been bruised by her brother's famous rages and whose lands had been especially hard hit by the enforced sharing out with Pelayo's intruders from the south. Amalsuntha had gauged which of the Astures saw themselves cheated of their deserved rewards from the riches of the great campaigns in the south in the early days. None of this had she forgotten and all of it she now poured into the eager ears of the African.

"The two of them ate, and drank, and coupled, and dreamed their separate dreams. Amalsuntha could foresee her return to the great world of the plains. The splendid buildings, the rich feasts, the gorgeous silks and the rich scents. A great stage on which to strut and to tantalize, to permit intimacy and to deny it. There would be many there who would appreciate the several attractions of a princess of the old blood. Her destiny was never here in the hills in the mud and the wood smoke, the brats and the toothless old women. This young man could take her south but men of greater power, greater wealth, greater needs would see to her fuller happiness there.

"Musa could see his dream materializing before him. The final pacification of the old kingdom of the Visigoths would be his. The last step—it had eluded so many—he would effect. Then they would know his true worth in Córdoba. And he would return with this golden one of silken body and silken hair. Men would envy him, admire her too. That is, if they could take their eyes from her brother in chains, or better, her brother's head upon a spear.

"Spies went out by night to the chiefs of the Astures laden with golden sacks and returned by night relieved of their burden. Though the weather began to improve none of the native bands visited the lands about Cangis. The huts of

Pelayo were mostly empty of visitors but in the bazaars outside of Gijón Asturian warriors drifted and spent more freely than people had known for long. Some of them entered the town itself and not too long after were seen to emerge unhurt, still armed, and to rejoin their companions and relatives.

"Then, when Bishop Oppa came up from the south to join the governor, it was decided that the time had arrived to throw the dice. The oily prelate of Toledo was himself the final gambit. As a Christian churchman, as a relative of the once Visigothic king Witiza, he demonstrated in his person that not all that much had changed in the south. That a reasonable man could still make his way with the Africans. That this skulking in the hills was as unnecessary as it was uncomfortable. He was empowered by Córdoba to offer amnesty and position to all Goths who would give up this rebellion. Pelayo could be included, even lead them south if he agreed. But, coached by Amalsuntha, neither man expected that. Better that he was deserted by his own men. Better yet that he was murdered by them. Only his head needs go south. Reinforced once more by Oppa's escort, the garrison marched west for Cangis de Onis.

"Of course they found it deserted. A few thin dogs prowled the empty huts and gardens. The curs tucked their tails and ran when the flames began to curl through the thatch and wattle. The great warrior had fled. They would have to send out scouting parties to find him and his fellow bandits. At least they would have to pretend to do that. Their spies, their friends among the Astures, had already betrayed him. A scarce five miles away Pelayo himself was hiding in a cave. He had gone to earth like a terrified rabbit. His back was to the mountains and all that was left now was to take his pelt. The handful of old supporters with him, his captains, could share in his death. The trap was ready to be sprung.

"The march to Covadonga was leisurely, even a parade. Five miles was not suffficient to raise a sweat. Supplies were few for the task was to be quick. Escape was impossible. The way in was easy but there was no way out for the fugitives.

"And there they were! High on the cliffside in a shallow hole! A cave hardly deep enough to hide their scanty numbers. Certainly not deep enough to offer much protection from arrows. It would not even accommodate food or supplies for more than a day or two. A child could see the hopelessness of their position. Still, it would be a hard scrabble up for the swordsmen to finish it. Better if they came down like lambs. Better—in the telling afterwards—if they were too terrified to resist even briefly. Musa offered a parley.

"Before their eyes the tall, heavily-muscled chieftain picked his way down the cliff face. He was armed, of course, but his sword was sheathed, his red hair bound for the fight but his shield above in the cave. Alone, by God! He had not lost the famous nerves of steel. To take him now would be simple but he reckoned they could not chance it. Pelayo knew that Musa would lose too much face, credit, with his own warriors and with those in Córdoba whose esteem he hoped to use subsequently when he had triumphed. Better to pass up the quick gain. The great warrior halted a few paces to their front.

"They had agreed that Oppa would conduct the parley. The bishop advanced now in turn.

"'Greetings, cousin. The years have dealt generously with you.'

"Pelayo never took his hard eyes from the group beyond the bishop.

"'And your new masters, cousin, have dealt generously with you. But doubtless you have served them well.'

"'We are not here, we have no time, to rub old wounds, Pelayo. Your fame is such that the whole of the southlands would make its peace with you. Now is the time for you to take advantage of it. This moment will pass, is passing even as we speak. The kingdom of the Goths which you defend is dead. Destroyed for its sins before our God and rightly so. It is not for a simple soldier, or even a chief, to dispute the judgment of our God. If our people will survive and one day flourish again, it will be because they have learned again to serve. This schooling under the Africans will be severe but need not be cruel. For those of the old leadership of the Goths who will take the first step in this needful penance a not ungenerous appreciation is sure. You and I, priest and soldier, know how to obey. We understand, each of us, the uses of obedience if anything is to be accomplished. We lead just because we understand that.

"'I can offer you now, Pelayo, the post of captain-general and of inspector of all of the Gothic forces which serve the emir at Córdoba. You have earned it. To the annual golden salary that accompanies those offices, the emir will add such estates outside of Córdoba as you yourself will select, up to a maximum of ten thousand acres. That is, complete with the buildings that stand upon them and the slaves that work them. You must swear a suitable oath of obedience to the emir, of course, and he is confident that, with a man of your honor, such an oath will secure him the peace of the realm on which security and prosperity for all of us will depend. He is even willing that you should retain those warriors who have followed you loyally here in the mountains. They can become your personal bodyguard in the south.

"'All this I can offer you here and now, Pelayo, but your

consent cannot be put off any longer. The alternative is war to the knife. It is a war, as you see, that you can only lose, today and in this place. Join me, and our people. Help to repair the injuries which their sins have visited on them. Do not further resist the deserved judgment of our God.'

"Saying this, Oppa extended his hand to Pelayo as if to seal the bargain. But the redhaired Goth continued to look beyond him at Musa and his officers. Not once thus far had the warrior deigned even to direct his gaze to the bishop. Now Oppa flushed, hesitated, and slowly withdrew his hand, as if seeking to disguise the fact that he had ever really offered it. Taking advantage, finally, of that humiliating moment, Pelayo looked directly at him and spoke. His words were heavy with scorn and anger yet they were spoken slowly and carefully, with full control as well as force.

"'You speak of the judgment of our God, bishop. Perhaps you should speak, rather, of the betrayal of our king. Does Christ work through subtle prelates who alienate their own chiefs from them? Do those who ease the invasion of foreigners, the subjugation of their own people, serve the divine purposes? And do those who serve in such a treason gain thereby the right to lead in the slavery they have plotted.?

"'You say that you can offer me a share in such a leadership. I say that I have already taken it. Look about you, bishop. When have you seen Goths and Astures united? When has anyone? And this has happened in freedom. We, all of us, are free and you come to offer us slavery? You ask me to join you as Judas goat and lead them into slavery. I will make you an offer instead, Oppa. You may surrender now and do penance with us in these mountains rather than with the Africans in the south. These African warriors who have escorted you can depart in peace if they do it now, immediately, and if they withdraw south of the mountains.

"'We will let them depart to the south which they hold for now. But we warn them as well, we shall come for them there too. This people whom I lead will become the masters of this entire land once again and their people will have to withdraw beyond the straits or they will die on the soil that they have seized through your treachery and that of your house. That is the will of our God, Oppa. And I pronounce it to you. Today is but another step in the liberation of the Gothic nation. Tell your masters that and I will wait their decision either for peace or for war.'

"Deliberately then, Pelayo turned his back on the bishop and began a slow climb towards the cave above. Oppa withdrew in confusion and anger to the party of Musa. They enjoyed his humiliation, he could see that. Most of all, the woman, Amalsuntha. The mockery was a scarcely disguised in her eyes. The bitch! She would see only a few more days of life than her arrogant brother if he could see to it.

"The African governor and his officers now withdrew into the front ranks of their troops. 'Have the archers open fire as soon as the red-haired sonofabitch reaches the cavemouth. Five gold tremises to the man who first punctures the big blowhard.'

"At the command, the front ranks nocked their arrows. It was not an easy shot but it was not an impossible one either. If they were to get full credit for the victory they needed to make a good show before the ballistas already being muscled up from the rear were brought into play.

"'Fire.' A sheet of arrows rose into air before the cliff face but Pelayo had already rolled forward and down into cover.

"'Rodrigo! Rodrigo!'

"The battlecry of these savages and bandits rose and

echoed. From the cliff-top above the cave a hail of arrows rose and plunged in return. The darts sunk into the close ranks of Musa's command on the valley floor striking here and rattling there. Those archers, who had waited to see the effects of their first volley, now hurriedly began to nock for a second. But even as they did so another rain of missles struck them from the hidden positions of their enemies above. They fired back while their fellows were falling, writhing and screaming. Suddenly, even the merest recruit could see that the contest had tilted to the enemy. It seemed for a moment that some magic had returned their own arrows against them—that the spirits were taking a hand. But the veterans knew. They had been led into a trap by their young commander. This was a killing ground and the stupid bastard had let himself be drawn onto it.

"At the same time, far behind them, Gijón was erupting into flame. Hours after the departure of Musa's troop a mixed force of Goths and Asturians had sprung from cover to race for its palisades. Once the scaling ladders had bumped against them, those flimsy walls had yielded to the hundreds of hands grasping their tops. The startled skeleton of the garrison left behind went down quickly before surprise and numbers. What had ensued was not so much a battle as a massacre. The attackers made no attempt to capture the little town but only to destroy it. Firebrands had been hurled from the first onto its roofs and into its huts and houses. In a nightmare of smoke and flame the town was emptied out. Of those who fled the flame, anyone with a weapon was cut down. The destruction was complete and utter. The meager defending force perished to a man as the fire drove them into the open.

"At Covadonga the ballistas had ground to a halt. Half the crew that manhandled them into place was bleeding on the ground. The other half desperately sought shelter under their own machines or behind them. And the cries of their officers could not move them from their refuges.

"Musa had already dispatched strong contingents to both flanks with orders to enfilade the enemy archers and to clear them from the heights overlooking the cave and valley floor. Now news was coming back that the slopes to the right and left seemed just as strongly held and that his troops, attempting to fight uphill, were being badly mauled and making but slow progress. The African commander could see that his force, with the exception of the artillerymen, continued to hold their formations and to return the fire of Pelayo's force. But they were being reduced increasingly to scavenging in the dirt for arrows or to wrenching enemy missles from the bodies of their own dead and even from the wounded. Only the volume of the enemy fire was keeping them supplied. Up on the cliff their attackers seemed to have an endless store of missles.

"So far they were subjected only to fusillades of arrows. The Goths were hoarding their spears and javelins for now. But none of the beleagured veterans was deceived as to the meaning of that. The bastards were saving the heavier stuff for the close. When enough of them were down, the survivors would see heavy weapons enough. More than any sensible soldier would have a taste for.

"Suddenly there was a lull in the discharges from above. As will the bravest of troops under fire, the African warriors began to slow their own response. Even the trained nerves of veterans cannot entirely resist the superstition that inaction somehow avoids provoking a response. At first no one on the valley floor understood what was happening although they were grateful for the respite. Then, one after another, they began to find their attention drawn to a strange drama unfolding at the very center of their own ranks.

"There the Gothic woman Amalsuntha and her old maid had shed their overcloaks to reveal splendid white linen and gold jewels. Each of them carried in her right hand an embossed steel dagger of the sort worn by the great. Into the quick silence, broken only by the high screams of the dying wounded, the blond princess raised her own voice in a shout.

"'You win again, brother. You refuse glory and wealth for all of our family, you great, stupid fool. You destroy our people. You mix our blood with the dirt and ignorance of these mountain peasants. Well, you will die. If not this time, the next one. Could I see it, I would spit on your corpse. But for now you will not have me to sacrifice to your filthy allies. A princess knows how to live. She knows how and when to die.'

"The women turned then to one another. Each placed the point of her blade against the chest of the other and encircled the other with her left arm. Then, with a motion which was at once a thrusting of her own body forward and clasping tight of the body of the other, they came together in violence. So passionate was that embrace that they seemed, for a moment after, almost to recoil from its contact. But they clasped one another even tighter in a frenzy of determination. Suddenly blood began to flow down between them and their grip on one another tightened yet more as they swayed and their legs began to buckle. They made no sound, the princess and her lady. Slowly, as if retiring on her couch once more, Amalsuntha sank backward, then pitched to the ground. Her ancient retainer fell upon her mistress's body as if to shield it to the last.

"Now, from the cliff above it came again, and this time with exultation. From hundreds of voices it came.

"'Rodrigo! Rodrigo! Rodrigo!'

"Musa knew that they must escape now. Pelayo's sister had destroyed more than herself and an idiot old maid. She had destroyed the will of his troops to resist. The most stupid of them knew that their commander's paramour had read the signs of disaster.

His luck was gone. If he did not begin to withdraw them now in an orderly fashion, it would take only the first of them to break to turn withdrawal into a rout. His men were brave, veterans, but superstitious as soldiers are.

"By now he had intelligence as well that the return route would be one long ambuscade. He could guess that should they manage to reach Gijón they would find it in the hands of the enemy.

Pelayo, who had contrived this trap so cleverly, would not have overlooked that. Daring and surprise in his turn was the only remedy. They would take to the hills themselves. They would retreat directly over the mountains.

"Sweating like a pig, he was everywhere directing his troops. They were startled but well satisfied to be breaking off this hopeless contest. Now the enemy would have to come to them. They would have to come out of their secure little hiding places and into the open. Not that they'd have much stomach for that. And they would have to form up and meanwhile we'll have a breather.

"Some of the veterans drew back momentarily at the turn into the hills. But again Musa was at them, threatening, shouting, striking. Discipline prevailed. And the idea that now they were sheltered, concealed, took hold—at least for the first few hours. The rearguard had little to do but fire at shadows. The enemy seemingly had no desire to fall upon them as they retreated up the valley.

"Towards dusk it began. The trees felled across the

obvious route, the jeers and then arrows from deeper in the forest pines, even an occasional javelin from some bandit, braver than the rest, who popped up and cast, then raced back into cover. One by one the native guides were picked off as they strove to direct the column up towards the ridgelines. The uneasy feeling began to grow that they were being herded—pushed by their enemies. That they were no longer headed for safety but rather into another trap. The wounded were being abandoned. Little groups were breaking off the column in futile attempts to escape the developing disaster.

"Everywhere the foe had the higher ground. Now rocks, hurled or rolled down, were becoming the major menace. Their number and volume increased as the terrain gave the Christians ever more superior position. Finally it seemed that the very mountain itself had begun to fall on them.

"At mid-morning of the second day all pretense of order, all discipline was lost. Attempting to halt the rout, Musa himself fell to a sudden thrust by one of his own and his remaining officers joined the blind flight. Now a mere terrified mob, what was left of the Gijón garrison was cut off, set upon, slain at every turn, in every place that they sought to find respite or momentary security. Finally, all was silence. There were no survivors. All that remained was carrion for the wolf, the wild pig, and the crows.

"Pelayo had the bodies of his sister and her maid buried in graves left unmarked, for there were many who could not forgive Amalsuntha even in death. Even though they knew now that the land was free. Even though they understood that the African would not come again to plant a garrison before their door. Pelayo calculated that his new people had been finally born in the bloodbath at Covadonga. There Visigoth and Asture had become something else. Whatever they were to become, they had been joined there once and for all. A new kingdom had been birthed. A new kingdom had triumphed."

* * *

Hafts of daggers and cups pounded on stools or shields. Whatever was in reach. The great old story had been told again. Gifts showered about the bard Favila, from every hand. The winter was ending. Lent was over. The Christ had risen. The raiding season would begin once more. Time to sober up—time to get back in shape for fighting. Time to leave the women and the kids. Time for glory and plunder. They loved it. They might not yet be sober but they were going to be, they told themselves. The old man could really tell the story and the old king could really throw a feast.

The general mood was so festive that the crowd even made way willingly for the young whelps of Alfonso pushing heavily towards the door. From the look of the one in the middle, Ramiro they called him, they'd had too much feasting themselves. Maybe they would get him outside before he threw up on his own feet and maybe they wouldn't. What the hell, royalty ought to be able to hold its booze.

Behind them, immobile on his throne, the face of Alfonso was black.

# Chapter Three

Nepotian hated these late Sunday-night dinners with their uncle. The purpose was so obviously to educate Ramiro, Aurelius, and himself in the ways of monarchy and politics. Old Alfonso alone, after the food, with his three nephews and possible heirs could pontificate as much as he chose. The absence of the magnates of the land—and even of the servants—enabled him to speak frankly. He did not have to attend to the sensibilities of the court and their own he frankly disregarded. Indeed, the latter he considered himself to be in the process of giving form.

Ramiro loves the sessions, of course. The Ram already regards himself as particularly chosen and any inclusion in the royal confidence makes him swell in importance just short of bursting like a toad. He is absurd in his self-regard. Aurelius is just the opposite. He is almost completely passive. He sits as still and quiet as the hare who hopes that the fox has not seen him. The baby among the three cousins appears to think that he is just some sort of necessary audience. He almost never ventures a comment or opinion and when the king requires one of him, Oro is seized with confusion. For all of that our old uncle thinks pretty well of him, so far as Nepotian can see.

Neppy's thoughts continued.... Sometimes they amuse me but, for the most part, the boredom is almost stupefying. It's hard to stay awake but it is dangerous to nod. I wouldn't mind if the old man could really see us as equals. If he would only tell us how he hopes to manage a succession in this spider web, the succession of any one of us, I could be interested. I believe that our uncle has things worth telling us. But he lectures us like children. Worse yet, now he's going to correct us like children.

And Nepotian was right. "Ramiro," the king was asking, "How are we to regard you as royal nephew and future king when you so cleverly seize upon solemn court occasions to get falling-down drunk? I am trying to establish you as an adult, a warrior, and a possible leader and you are acting the child. Do you know how many enemies we have? Does it amuse you to go on handing them the dagger they will use on your throat?"

For not the first time that night, Ramiro reddened to the point of apoplexy. He stammered when he was taken off guard.

"No, uncle. I'm sorry, uncle. I won't do it again."

Scarcely taking heed of the youth's words, the king continued.

"Must I draw you a picture, all of you? My noble lords and bosom companions charge me with prolonging the childhood of the lot of you. They say that you need a taste of the real camp life, of campaigning. They want me to let you in particular, Ramiro, march out with them for the south this spring so that you can get some experience in war. You'd like that, wouldn't you? But am I supposed to trust you with them? I know that I can't trust them—or most of them. The real question is whether or not I can rely on you.

"Let me tell you how it will go, Ramiro, this first blooding of the royal nephew. They'll get you experience all right. They'll see that you're kept safe even as you're being blooded. They'll feed you a few not too-talented or already-wounded Africans. At night they'll drink with you and tell you what a great warrior you are ready to become. They'll find you a captive woman or two. Then, when the time is right, when you are fuddled and full of yourself, they'll ask you for certain assurances. They won't talk outright rebellion of course. Nothing that you could put a finger on. Just some guarantees of land and titles when you've become my heir are all that they'll ask. A little for this one, and a little more for that one.

"Are you ready for that? Can you deal with them? If you're too curt, too stiff, you will come home on your shield. Stiff forever. 'Poor Ramiro! He would have made a doughty king! We tried everything we could to save him but his valor outran his experience!' We'll bury you with royal honors."

Alfonso mimicked, letting his voice drip scorn. He paused, and then went on.

"How good a liar are you? Can you dissemble with men who are born dissemblers themselves? Who will you play against whom? Who will you let go to an 'honorable death'—and so demonstrate to the others that it is possible to go beyond the proper limits in this game? Who will you pick to guard your back and how will you reward him for adhering to your party? How far into treason will you take yourself to ensure my peaceful demise and your eventual succession?"

Ramiro was overcome with confusion. He could not think what his uncle wanted him to say. His uncle, the king.

"I would not betray you, uncle! I would never do that!"

Ramiro knew that he was missing the mark. He knew that his uncle wanted something more but he could not think what it was. He hated this toying with words. Why wouldn't the old man simply tell him.

"Then you are of no use to me, nephew. You are no use dead. I do not have an heir of my body so you will have to bid for the crown against your cousins here. And I can be but one of the arbiters. That is the trap that my obedient subjects have woven for me. Or perhaps that I once wove for myself. It hardly matters. The important thing is that you understand the game, that you master the game. And I am not sure that you are ready to string your bow for it."

"But Uncle," Nepotian broke into the silence that threatened to prolong itself uncomfortably, "Ramiro cannot learn to manipulate the magnates until you take the risk of letting him try. None of us can. And while you hold us back from trying, your enemies, our enemies, accuse you of keeping us children just to protect your throne. Or worse."

Alfonso regarded the young man in silence for a moment. He gave the appearance of considering his words. When he spoke his voice was low, almost inaudible, but cutting.

"My, my. You are clever, Nepotian. We all know it, don't we boys? Will you read the old fox a lesson or are you just showing off for your cousins' benefit? Don't be obvious. Don't make me think less well of you."

The king directed his gaze to Aurelius then.

"What about you, Oro? You're the youngest pup. Still, you showed the other night that you think yourself man enough to hold great quantities of wine. And then you and Nepotian managed to carry Ramiro here outside to do his puking in at least semi-privacy. You tell us what it is that we are trying to protect, trying to hand on here."

"The kingdom, Uncle!" Oro blurted it out even as he knew that it was not the answer. Even as he realized that the king did not expect him to know the answer.

"Indeed, Aurelius. And what is that?" The king blocked his line of escape from their attention.

"The kingdom of the Visigoths, sir! The kingdom refounded by Pelayo and passed on to you from your father, Fruela. The leadership of our people."

The king smiled and turned towards the fire. He showed them his back. Quietly, he seemed to speak to the embers themselves.

"How grandly you put it, Oro. So that is what you all would have. Our people. Asturian peasants and bandits. Gothic refugees and warriors. All of us holding this rain-besotted earth, scratching out beans, gathering apples and acorns. And for honor, and proof of manhood, and some excitement to hide us from our real selves, stealing south in little parties to murder and rape and plunder the Africans." I have done that. I have done all of that. I have been a great sacker of cities, a torcher of fields, and a slaughterer of cattle and sheep as well as men. All the way to the Atlantic and through the flatlands across the mountains down even to the Duero River and beyond.

"When I'm dead the bards will chant their tales of me for bigger fools to drink by. But I'll be no less dead, no less mouldering for all their songs. To what end?"

"Uncle," Ramiro burst out, "The Africans would do the same to us. They try to do the same to us every year."

"Yes," Alfonso replied, "And so it goes on—so far. Perhaps you are ready to lead, Ramiro. You seem to think with your sword arm.

"But have you counted the odds? Maybe I should send you south to see Córdoba. What's the point, boy? Do you really think that old King Rodrigo sleeps somewhere in the hills? That he will come again to restore the kingdom of the Goths? That was a trick, boy. In the old days Pelayo played it in desperation and it worked. But that magic wore off long ago. The kingdom of the Goths is dead. It has been for a hundred years. No one of us here but that has as much Asturian blood as Gothic, maybe more. And the Astures, in the old days, had no love for the Goths."

The king gazed at the three cousins. They avoided his look but did not glance at one another either.

"What is it that you would do if you did become king? Does any one of you have a thought in your brain that goes beyond whoring and killing and drinking?"

Finally, it was Nepotian who answered. But after a pause in which the fire cracked and glowed and cast its lights on the royal plate and goblets still scattered about the board. He was still smarting from the earlier rebuke and hoped to avoid another.

"We would try to continue what you have done, uncle. You have built so many churches. The old goblins and witches of the countryside have fewer followers every year. You have had the old Massbooks of the Christians of the south brought north and copied. The priests make us one people every Sunday. We all say the same prayers and they all bless the same king.

"And you have had the old lawbook of the Goths copied as well. The laws from the south teach the glory of a land where the king rules and the people live in justice."

Nepotian watched anxiously as, finally, his uncle smiled a bit. Smiled and spoke a little wearily.

"Sometimes, Nepotian, I have some hope for you. You have a quick mind—although I am not sure that you have so quick a heart."

"Yes, Pelayo had a plan. Marriage and religion. A new people, one people, born out of the mingling of blood and the rule of a single faith. He may not have known it then but the boy, Sunna, that he had brought north with him turned out to be the most influential member of his war party. When

Sunna was a very old man and the chief priest of the court I knew him a little. He was almost as much the king as the king himself.

"And so I have followed Pelayo's lead. I build churches, splendid churches to catch the minds of the people, and I find priests for them. More than that, I have had a bishop of our own made for Oviedo, and another in Lugo and still another in Iria Flavia by the Atlantic's edge. The bishops of the southlands truckle too much to the plans of the African emir in Córdoba. And so we have a brave Christian church of our own through all these northern mountains.

"And I have made some of those dirty brawlers, my faithful chiefs and heads of clans, 'counts' in my own rich new palace. I have given them titles from the old days and new cloaks of fine silks brought up from the south. Pearls before swine!"

The king paused anew. He rose and walked back and forth in front of the fireplace. He was tall, Alfonso was. It was joked that if he rode any but the largest horse, his toes trailed in the dust. Yet he was thin—thin and a little stooped. The black of his hair and beard, the deep bronze of his skin, blended with the somber clothes that he habitually wore. Strangers thought him first a sort of monk, but his war chiefs feared him as a fighter. They had seen him kill.

"Do you think, boys, that many of those selfish, stinking louts are capable of realizing that only such a dream makes them more than animals? Do you believe that they would follow me as they do if I were not more savage than they? If I give them blood, gold, and women, then I am king. You think that I am king because old Bishop Adulfo poured holy chrism on my head? Do they love me because I build churches?

"You have heard what they did once to me. Ordoño,

Ermegildo, Teudemiro, Gondemaro, and the rest. They used your great-uncle Aurelius as a pawn to force me to retire to a monastery. They let me keep my life at the price of swearing a vow of perpetual chastity. Then when they tired of his weakness they allowed me to return since I could not father a successor. I have made them bleed for it and the people have turned me into some sort of idol. A king who does not use their women! But no one of my chiefs would tolerate an attempt of mine to marry now. They put it about—when they dare—that I prefer young boys. But what "they really fear is that I yet might marry and sire a son of my own.

"So my fine counts measure my days, take my victories, and come to my feasts. They even follow me to church on holy days. But they measure my days exceedingly finely. They look to play one of you off against the others when I am gone. They plan to swell their properties and nurse their own bastards by your sweat. Pursuing their petty aims and greeds they would bring this little land to fire and sword. They have no vision.

"And that, my nephews, is why you are here. I will find one of you who will be more than their equal. I will put steel in his bones, in his blood. I will find a way to do that, believe me! You three have been friends in your childhood—as much as most anyway. But I doubt that you can continue to be. One of you is destined to be king. And the others? Will they survive the winner's succession? Likely not. Monasteries are handy places for potential rivals but people sometimes come back from the cloister. Look at me!

"You are in a contest, you cousins. Your own blood has marked you for it. And I? I, the king, have no intention of letting you escape your destiny! When the time comes, I will make a choice of one of you, and that same choice will probably be the death of the other two. This I must do. I cannot spare you such a fate. So think on the contest! Leave off this childishness!"

Abuptly the king wheeled and strode from the chamber. While the young cousins still sat, transfixed, the servants entered and began to clear the great table. Then they rose, each one, to go to find their own bedding. They did not speak to one another. They hardly dared to look at one another. But the silence followed them and pressed down on them until, finally, they slept.

# Chapter Four

"Look what you're doing. You're slopping the wineskin all over."

"I'm the one who stole it. If I spill it it's none of your Goddam business, Neppy."

The Ram was like a wounded bear tonight. He had been since they'd gotten there. Perhaps he was not so sure he hadn't been seen making off with the wineskin. Oro was uneasy himself. Maybe this little council of war was not so good an idea as it had seemed. Maybe the whole thing was best let lie for a while. Still, when Nepotian had suggested it both he and Ramiro had thought at first that it seemed like the kind of thing they ought to do.

The little lean-to was in surprisingly good shape still. The wattle walls and thatching offered plenty of shelter for this kind of mild spring night. They hadn't lit a fire, for attention was just what they wanted to avoid. From within the forest edge where they had sited it the outlying huts of Oviedo were not more than a healthy bow-shot away. Any one of the old folks coming out to relieve himself might easily catch sight of a fire. By now, anyway, the glow from the wine was beginning to make them insensible to the slight freshness of the night breeze.

The shelter was only the most recent and the only survivor

of a long line of such lean-tos that the three of them had built in the forests around the town. This one was now, Oro would guess, about three or four years old. They hadn't visited it in almost two years. Not unless Neppy and Ram had come without him—and he doubted that. Still, they were a little awkward with one another. When they were younger it was a spot to bring and share the things they managed to steal from their uncle's kitchen, or from the stable, or from the armory.

They could lounge about there and lie about the deer that they were going to kill. Or about the rabbit, or the squirrel, that they had actually trapped. It was a place to speculate together about what girls really felt like. How soft were they down there? Did they really like it or did they only do it to get babies? More timidly, they could broach the subject with one another of whether they would be scared when their first battle came. Were the old warriors scared anymore? Was moss really good for sword wounds? What would you do if you lost an arm?

But Ramiro was seventeen now. He had killed his deer and was always talking about his first campaign to come. If Neppy could be trusted, the Ram had already laid with a woman, maybe three or four. Oro hadn't known it until the other day when Nepotian had blurted it out. It was more difficult now for them to talk. Oro had come to dislike always being the baby. Hell, he was fifteen. Oro pondered the situation.... Anyway, my two cousins have taken to hanging around the warriors. The three of us have just sort of let the old secret meetings in the woods drop.

At least until the other night. Our uncle really threw a scare into all of us—even if we are not going to put it that way. When Nepotian suggested that we meet tonight and talk about our own plans for our future it had sounded very adult. It was so daring an idea that a small thrill coursed down all of our backs, probably. At least it did down mine. Why should we let our uncle tell us how we were going to act? We can work out our own futures! We are the heirs to the kingdom!

But each of us knows that this is treason. We won't say that out loud to one another either. But that's the thrill of it. That's why Ramiro stole the wine. We came to celebrate our own daring—our defiance of the old king. The only thing is—we're fighting among ourselves.

"Sure it's his business, Ramiro. It's mine too. That's the point. We're all together because we all have the same problem. We need to be able to speak up to one another if something is wrong. Otherwise we'll end up fighting among ourselves. We'll just prove that our uncle is right."

"Okay, Oro, okay. I know that as well as you do. But everybody has his own talent, you know? I can take a chance and get away with it. Carry it off. You or Neppy would have gotten caught. You would have given yourself away. Neither of you is bold enough. So give me a little credit for that. Don't nag me about it if I slop some of it around. I can't be an old lady. It's not my nature."

"We're not going to work anything out if we start calling names, Ramiro. Oro has a point. The fix we're in is not the sort of thing that is solved by charging at it headlong. We can't put an arrow in it and then bury it. All three of us have to respect one another. Those of us who are better at planning will have to be listened to."

"And that means you, Neppy, right?" Ramiro's mood was not getting any better. He knew it himself but his cousins were ganging up on him. They had always done that. He took the chances and they got the benefit. More than that, dammit, they told him how they would have done it. Shit!

Oro was becoming more and more worried. This wasn't going right at all. Ramiro and Nepotian had often fought and sooner or later they wanted him to take sides.

"Maybe we should save the rest of the wine until we talk this thing out."

"Look, Oro, if you'll just drink your share then you won't have to worry about me getting drunk." Ramiro shoved the wineskin at Aurelius. "If you're going to be grown up, like the rest of us, you're going to have to pull your own load, kid. What we're going to need before everything else is nerve. If you can't even hold your own drink what good are you to the rest of us?"

Oro took the wineskin and tipped it into his mouth, letting the biting fluid slide down his throat without swallowing. He had seen the older warriors do it. He knew that this piece of bravado was not a good idea—he already felt a little light-headed—but he needed to show Ramiro. He was a man too.

"Don't keep picking on Oro, Ram." Nepotian thought that he'd better keep his older cousin from bullying the kid into getting thoroughly loaded. If we're going to be a team, if we're going to hold together, we have to watch out for one another."

"And that's the point, Neppy, that's the point. Every team has a leader. In a war party, or even a hunt, only one man can be in charge. To take care of the others. And if he's going to take care of them, they have to learn how to take orders. When he says they're too far out front, they have to come back. When he says they're too far back, they have to catch up. Otherwise, it's not a war party anymore. It's just a bunch of kids out playing soldier. Then somebody gets killed. Or maybe everybody gets killed."

Nepotian could feel himself getting a little heated. After

a while, Ramiro usually had this effect on him. Just because the Ram had muscles to spare he seemed to think that they were the most important thing in the world. If he could, he'd use them to think with. Still, a shouting match wasn't going to get them anywhere. He tried to control his own voice and the effort made it a little squeaky. Damn!

"All right, Ramiro. We both know that you're right. No body is going to argue about that. But ruling a kingdom is more than just waging a war. And, after all, wars are fought at particular times and in particular places. Even for particular reasons. You are probably the best warrior of the three of us and likely always will be. So you will probably always lead when the business is actual fighting. But for deciding when a fight is necessary or if we can win, that takes more than one head. And three heads are better than one."

"If there is time for that, Neppy, if there is time." Ramiro had the advantage and was warming to his subject. He felt good, confident, but he was sure that he wasn't drunk. It was just that it was time to let Nepotian and Oro know what they were really talking about.

"But there is such a thing as leadership, you know. I mean, thinking something out is important, but things come up suddenly and you just have to react. There are times when the only chance you have to win is to take it to the enemy all at once—while they think that you are still talking. You push them into a corner, you knock them over, before they're set.

"Now knowing when that moment has come, knowing when your enemy has relaxed his sword-grip. That's what kingship is about. There is no substitute for it. That's why everyone, even the toughest of the nobles, is scared of our uncle. He has it. You don't see them arguing with him."

Ramiro was sure that he had scored. He had carried the argument. He was more than a little flushed and leaked a small smile of self-satisfaction despite himself.

Nepotian answered with more heat than he intended. "And you see where our uncle is. He can't even pick his own successor. We've been forced on him instead of his own flesh and blood. And he won't even get a free choice among us. Sure he's tough, a real killer. But somewhere back there he made a mistake that he couldn't undo. He gave his enemies a handle that not all his toughness can overcome.

"If rulers were just lions, you'd be the greatest lion of them all, Ramiro. But to rule a kingdom, you have to do the right favors for the right people. You have to give out lands and take away lands. You have to build churches here and not there. You have to let this one marry that heiress, and forbid that one to marry his daughter to this heir. It's not so much a battle as it is a chess game, Ramiro—and that game goes to the one with the most patience, with the most cunning."

"And that's you, isn't it, Neppy? The great know-all, the big mind! But for all those cute little games you like to play, the first real necessity is to be able to face men down. Real men! If you don't win that first contest, you don't even get to play the others. Raw courage is the prime talent—that and a sense of timing. Do you think that you or Oro could match me at that?"

Aurelius was feeling a little sad and maybe a little sick as well. He had only been sipping at the wineskin but even so he was belching more and more. And with each belch he was more apprehensive that he would begin to puke. It hadn't happened yet but the nausea he was feeling made him worry that it would.

Then too, he had the feeling that Nepotian and Ramiro were leading up to a real fight. It would be like the ones they'd had often enough in the old days but now they were grown. What might come of a fight between them now worried him. Abruptly he got to his feet. He wasn't too steady.

"Listen, we had better think about this some more and talk about it another time. If we're away from the palace any longer we'll be missed."

"Feeling your booze, cousin? You look a little wobbly. Maybe Nepotian should help you back." Ramiro could not resist the jibe.

"No. No, we had better go back one by one. Just the way we came. We don't want people asking us what we were doing.

"I'll go first." And without waiting for an answer, Oro turned and started off into the dark. He wasn't sure that he was going to be sick but he sure as hell wasn't going to be sick in front of them.

The moon had not yet risen. The darkness was near stygian among the huts of Oviedo. Darkness cast a shadow in this fetid closeness. Oro breathed a silent prayer that he wouldn't run into a hound. Christ! The last thing he wanted was to run into some half-wild cur. He didn't even have a good kick left in him. He just wanted to get someplace where he could lie down. Someplace where he could close his eyes. Just a solid, quiet place to slow his gurgling stomach.

He took the deepest breaths he could. He trailed his outstretched hand just along the fibered wattle walls. Not so hard as to wake anyone. Just enough to steady himself. For a sense of balance.

"Aaaagh!" He was falling half sideways. His left hand groped for support but the darkness yielded before his grasp. The wall was gone. Had he tripped? No. He had bumped into something—someone? No, by God, he had been pushed! Or had he?

The throbbing in his head began to ease a bit and his orientation started to return. The darkness was still total but he became slowly aware of a heat beside him. He listened and heard breathing other than his own.

Almost as soon as he reached out and touched whatever it was the touch was returned. A hand on his skin—on his face—on his .... Dear God, it was a girl! A naked woman! Pulling at him now, thrusting between his legs! Pressing herself close against him. Her nakedness against his now!

Then the screaming began. Right in his face. The shrillness of it made him recoil drunkenly. It hurt his head. And her nails were raking his face. This was no dream—no nightmare. He could feel the blood starting. He tried to push back—to push her back—but she was strong, this one, whoever she was. She continued to claw at his face and chest. He could feel the welts springing up.

"Murder! Murder! Rape! He wants to murder me." She was screaming now at the top of her lungs.

Then there was a light. Someone had a lamp, a torch. His head was jerked back violently. They were trying to pull him up by his hair. He fumbled with his hands for purchase on the dirt. He tried to bend his knees.

"Wait! Wait a minute, for God's sake! I'll get up! I'll get up!"

But other hands joined those tangled in his hair. They pulled at his arms and at his shoulders. The hut was full of people, men shouting at him. They had him up, shoving him from one to the other.

"Kill the bastard! Dirty little lecher! Is the girl all right?"

"Not his fault if she is! Tore her clothes right off, he did! Bruises all over her body. Good thing she fought back."

"Here's a fat bruise for you, lover boy! A fist thudded into the side of his head. Something—the flat of a sword—hit square across his back. He was reeling again. Then a knee plowed hard into his abdomen. Oro began to retch, and retch again. The sour wine burned up his throat. It stung his nostrils. He thought he was going to choke and gasped to get his breath—only to retch again. He could not clear his throat. He was going to die—to choke on his own vomit.

He could not make out a face. The hut was whirling about him. He staggered, dripping blood and puke. Then he could feel himself falling. He hit the dirt of the floor. Feet pummeled his sides. He was drifting away from them. Through the mist of pain he heard it.

"This is the son-of-a-bitch who thought he'd be king someday?"

They knew who he was!

# Chapter Five

The king's private chamber had an exotic atmosphere. Its small dimensions appeared even smaller because of the tapestries that hung about every wall. Gorgeous silks from the Arab south, done in golden and silver threads, they caught the swelling and falling light of the fire and had an almost hypnotic effect upon the unwary eye. But there was almost nowhere else to look—for all of them felt their presence in the royal chamber a strange thing. Ordinarily only the body-servants of Alfonso moved here but the king had decided that the inquest should be held in privacy. It involved his own nephew.

That meant there were too many people in such a confined space, of course. The girl and her father, she on a small stool and he standing, were to the left of the king. It appeared that her mother had been dead for some years. Against her nervous pallor the bruises of the young woman's face stood out starkly. She kept her head well down to avoid any glances at all and her hands twisted nervously in her lap. Her father shifted his weight back and forth. He struggled to look indignant, outraged, but now and again a look of something like terror flitted across his face. He sweated, perhaps not solely because of the heat and closeness of the room.

Opposite them stood Aurelius. No seat for the accused.

His face was as well marked as the girl's. But it was swollen to boot. One eye was almost invisible. Apart from that his bearing was composed enough, the king thought. Two days had been allowed for his recovery from the major effects of the beating he had received and it was clear that no bones had been broken. Nevertheless, the young man still had about him the faint air of someone recently aroused from sleep—bewildered and not yet convinced that his predicament was actual rather than a persisting dream.

The king himself was entirely clad in black. Not a single ornament tempered his attire. The effect was to suggest a royal executioner, which impression was precisely what he intended. It, and the fierceness of his long face and dark, piercing eyes, made his presence menacing to all of them. No one was exempt from the suggested threat of the royal mien.

Alfonso could not really believe that Oro had attempted the rape of which he now stood accused. The boy was too soft, too timid, for one thing, despite all the usual self-enhancing bluster of the budding young. Then again, there was something fine in his makeup, too fine maybe for the role that his birth had set him. Even stupid drunk, it was difficult to imagine him as a rapist. Yet the boy was hiding something. He was evasive. The king had no clear idea of what had happened and that worried him.

And so he had adopted the most severe of his masks. Fright, he had often found, was more likely to produce a hidden truth than friendly persuasion. Some of those here were certainly lying, perhaps all of them were in some measure. If he could throw all of the weight of outraged royalty into the scales possibly one or more of them would collapse under the pressure and the real truth begin to emerge. It was the best he could do for his nephew. But a scare wouldn't hurt Oro either. And those two sanctimonious cousins of his, Ramiro and Nepotian, on his flanks at the moment but perhaps belonging out there with Aurelius. He had not seen the two of them so close in months. They were implicated in this business somehow though they denied any connection with it. Nor had Oro involved them. Damn!

Between the girl and her father and Aurelius on the other side were his counselors. Counts Scipio, Ordoño, and the rest, they craned and rocked and murmured asides, one to the other. The king could not resist the fleeting thought that they were for all the world like vultures around a carcass. But whose? Aurelius' or his own? How much advantage would they dare to take? Certainly they would twist this mess to discredit him if that were possible. Did they really give a moldy sausage for Oro's plight—or the girl's for that matter? One thing was obvious. They would use this little judicial stage to strut and preen, even jostling one another if they could make pleasing their king work to their own advantage, however momentary.

He cleared his throat and the murmurs died away. "Look at me, girl. I'm going to ask you some questions and I want to see your face and your eyes when you answer me. The truth now! I can have them bring in the Holy Book for you to swear upon if I begin to think that you're lying to me. Now tell me what went on the other night."

"I was almost raped, my lord."

Alfonso regarded her somberly for a minute. No, she was too young, too frightened to be playing a game with him.

"We know what the charges are, child. Tell us how all this came about. Tell us about that evening. Tell us how it was that you were alone at night."

"Because my father went out to a friend's hut. He likes to go there to drink with his friends."

She stopped in a little confusion. Her father was glowering at her. Perhaps she should not have said that just so? She hurried on.

"I mean he doesn't always. Only sometimes. More since Momma died. He always comes home the same night."

There was a small buzz of amusement. The king broke in upon it hastily.

"So since your father left you alone regularly at night a man could have expected to find you so?"

"Yes, my lord. Or I suppose so."

"And did men ever visit you at night when your father was not there?"

"No, my lord."

"Did this young man," indicating Aurelius with a wave of his hand, "ever visit you there before?"

"No, my lord, never."

"Had you ever seen him before that night?"

"Yes, my lord. I had seen him about the streets and once or twice with you yourself when there were processions through the streets of the town or in church."

"And did he see you? Did he ever speak to you?"

"I don't know, my lord. Surely he never spoke to me. Not to a poor common girl like myself."

Alfonso was troubled. He sensed that the girl was not lying. Not so far. Her manner was too matter-of-fact for that. There had to be more to this.

"So you were alone at home. And suddenly he broke in upon you. Were you asleep? Tell me what happened and how."

"I was still awake, my lord. I was abed, waiting for my father to come home. And suddenly he," with a subdued gesture towards Aurelius, "dropped on top of me. I tried to raise up and he whispered that he would kill me if I made a sound. He tore my tunic from top to bottom and started to lick my nipples. I began to scream as loud as I could and I hammered at his head and face. I scratched his cheeks. I would have clawed his eyes out if I could. He struck me back. He slapped my face. I don't know how long we struggled before my father and some of his friends rushed in and pulled him off me. I am still sore, my lord, but he didn't rape me. He didn't have time. I think that he might have killed me."

The girl subsided into silence. She sat perfectly still without raising her eyes again. A small tremor passed through her body.

It has the ring of truth Alfonso thought, but still I find it hard to see my nephew so. Even in hot blood, even drunk besides. He turned to Aurelius who sat staring at the girl. What was her name—Toda? She hadn't mentioned Oro by name. No slips there. Would the boy do as well?

"Now it is your turn to tell us what happened, Aurelius. Did you know this woman before that night? Did it happen just the way she tells it?"

Aurelius shook his head, as if to dislodge a mist, and cleared his throat with a cough. He spoke low and hesitantly.

"I never saw her before, my lord. I never knew her. Some of what she said happened. Not exactly though. Not just the way she said it did."

Among the king's counselors there was a murmuring and a shifting. It seemed unbelievable but the boy was going to convict himself. Alfonso was dismayed. What had his nephew been about? What could he be thinking of?

"Did you try to force yourself on her, Aurelius, try to rape this young woman? You were in the hut. There are all sorts of witnesses to that. Your own bruises witness to it. Why were you there if not?"

"I was in the hut, lord. I was on my way back to the palace. It was late and I was a little drunk—more than a little drunk, I guess. The moon had not come up yet and it was very dark. I couldn't see well. Someone—something—pushed me through the door of her hut. I couldn't see who. When I fell she was just there."

There were titters in the audience and a muffled guffaw in the rear. The king groaned to himself. What was the young fool saying? If it had been a man he did not know so well telling such a tale he would have laughed outright himself. Yet Oro seemed earnest—sincere. There was no help but to go on with it.

"So you were drunk and just fell on her accidently? Is that it? You never tried to rape her?"

"I never did, my lord. It may have seemed so to her." He glanced at Toda almost anxiously but she, downcast still, was unaware of his mute appeal. "When I fell on top of her, no, next to her, I think, she had no clothes on. At least, I don't think she had. I couldn't feel any."

Now there was outright laughter in the chamber. The king glared about and it subsided but the smiles persisted. Alfonso couldn't blame them.

Aurelius hurried on, blushing now in the conciousness of what he had blurted out. "I mean, I was drunk. Maybe I was wrong. She could have thought that I was trying to attack her. I tried to push away. I was confused. She certainly did hit at me. She raked my face with her nails. But I just tried to push her off. No, I tried to push myself off. But I don't remember that I struck her. I don't think that I would have—that I did. Then the hut was full of torches and men and they punched me and kicked me until I fainted."

The king let the ensuing silence rest for a moment or two. He did not understand what was happening here. It was almost as if the two young people were playing a game with the rest of them. But it was a deadly game potentially. A menace hung in the air. There was an expectancy of blood about in the room.

"Then you and this young woman agree on much of what happened that night. But she says that she was clothed and you tore them off her, that you struck her, and that you tried to force yourself on her. You, on the other hand, deny that you had any criminal intent. You think that you did not strike her and you think that she was, in fact, naked. Neither one of you seems to know exactly how you found your way into her hut. You must know how ridiculous all of this sounds. Do you expect any of us to believe you, Aurelius? What were you doing there? Where had you come from?"

"I was coming from the forest, my lord. I had been there drinking and I had had enough. I was going back to the palace, as I told you."

"You were drinking alone at night in the woods? Why would you do that? Where did you get the wine? Who sold it to you?"

"I just took the wine, my lord. From the palace stocks. No one saw me. I suppose that I was unhappy and I wanted to feel better."

For the first time the king was absolutely sure that Oro was lying to him. The boy was no more a thief than he was a brooder. Most of the time he was the happiest of the cousins. Anyway his whole demeanor had changed. He was having trouble keeping his gaze even, his hands still.

"Now you're lying to me, boy. Do you know what these people here are thinking? Do you know what I think? Let me tell you what you did, you and this girl here."

At his words the girl looked up, startled, and her father—what was the man's name?—registered some sort of obscure emotion. Fright? It might be that he had more to hide than the girl or Aurelius. This might be getting somewhere.

"I think that you and she had made a little arrangement. She knew that her father was going out. You knew how to get your hands on a wineskin. So you were having a little party, the two of you, and unhappily her father came home early. She panicked and started to scream rape. And you? You got the senses beaten out of you before you had a chance to explain. Not that anyone would have believed you, under the circumstances. Isn't that what happened? Isn't that the truth of it? All hot blood and young love!"

He watched them both carefully. This was the way out of it.

He was giving them both the best chance to clear this mess. They were both lying to him. Well let them agree on a convenient lie and have done with it!

But the girl's eyes went to her father. His face was black. She began to shake her head no.

"No, uncle. I don't know her. That's not the way it happened."

Goddamn it! His hunting dogs made more sense than his nephew. Didn't he have any idea of the course that matters were taking? Count Scipio's eyes were on the boy, speculative, appraising him as victim? Only Aurelius appeared to have no idea of the danger now implicit in the proceedings.

"So you will persist in lying to me? I cannot believe your story and you have no other. The girl says that you attempted to rape her and you were taken in what seems to have been the very act. If all that stands you must know the penalty. Rape or attempted rape, the law makes no difference, of a virgin is punishable by death."

There was a strangled noise beside him. He half-turned to see that Ramiro was blurting something. Sweat was running down that young man's face and it sounded as though his nephew must choke.

"Toda is no virgin, my lord. She's no virgin!"

The king rounded on him. "You know that for sure? Have you yourself taken her?"

"No, my lord, but I know some who have. And not by force either. I can produce them if I can have a day."

There was a muffled exclamation and the girl's father turned on her. She shrank a little more. "Liar! Whore!" His fist caught her full in the mouth, smashing her lips against her teeth. She toppled backward from the stool and her skull made a dull sound as it struck the stone floor.

"Treason! Treason!" Count Ordoño already had a stiletto bright in his hand. Now he plunged it once, twice, rapidly into the neck of the girl's father. The man jerked, spasmodically, his legs stiffened in the effort to keep his balance. Then, his life's blood spouting from the gaping hole, he dropped to his knees, his body bent forward from the waist until his own forehead lay against the floor. He seemed to be asking the forgiveness of his daughter who lay there shrilling incomprehensibly. Then the victim's bowels burst and the air was suddenly full of the smell of sickly-sweet decay.

The count had dropped his bloody blade onto the floor at his own feet. "To offer violence in the presence of the king is treason, my lord. The room is small. I thought you might have been next. The man was mad!"

"Get him out! Get that piece of carrion out of the chamber! The girl too. And take my nephew under guard! All of you out! Except my counselors."

* * *

The king came to him in the early hours of the morning. Aurelius awoke immediately. His heart was pounding but he knew the instant of waking that he must make no sound. His uncle's hand on his shoulder told him not to rise.

"We're in a pretty mess, nephew."

The tone told Oro that his uncle had reached a decision and that somehow he was not being held responsible. Or not entirely responsible anyway.

"There has been a treason, a plot, and it will be a time before we can see what its intent was. The girl's father was in it but not of his own choice. He was nobody. But his mouth is shut. I don't know whether we'll ever get the truth from the girl. She's in some kind of trance. Maybe from fear, maybe from the blow on the head, maybe from seeing her father cough up his life on the floor in front of her.

"In any event, you stand as good as convicted of attempted rape. Virgin or not—did you ever think your randy cousin would stand you in good stead?—that is serious business. But I don't think that you did it. I'm not even sure that you were the intended target of the whole affair. But you surely made a great victim. A real lamb. You could hardly have helped them more.

"As it is, your innocence, combined with your stupidity, has left me no choice. I must at least appear to be executing justice in the sight of the people. I must a least appear to have been duped in the eyes of the conspirators. The hunt has only begun again and we need to leave a false spoor for the foxes.

"I'm going to exile you."

Aurelius gave a start but his uncle's hand pressed firmer against his chest.

"There is no appeal. My counselors, some of whom are certainly among the conspirators, have agreed that will be adequate punishment. Since you're of royal stock they do not insist on mutilation. For the same reason they will not insist on a full public trial. Indeed, they can't. They've already destroyed the best part of the evidence. But they think that I will exile you to Córdoba in the south. Then they can dicker with the emir there and play him and you against me if that seems desirable. On the other hand, I have no desire to give him or them such a counter.

"So I'm sending you to Galicia. There is a distant cousin of yours, a count, there who is sometimes loyal to me. I have his name in this little bag that I will give you. You are not to look at it until you are safely out of my territories. The bag also contains one of my small signet rings. You will use it to identify yourself to him—to prove that you're not just another adventurer. He will care for you, I hope, until I can recall you. But the whole thing may take some time to unravel."

The king's voice dropped, became huskier. "It is possible that I may never unravel it. For God's sake, Oro, try to think like a man. Try to realize that you have enemies—that you always will have. Royal blood is always a danger. Even your friends will try to use you. I will myself if I have to. The count to whom I send you will seek to use you as well. As of this moment you are a man, whatever you were before. I'm pushing you out of the nest. Fly like hell because lots of hawks are going to try their skills on you.

No! Don't say anything at all. When I leave, give me a minute or two. Then follow the scullery passage to the outside. Ramiro and Nepotian will meet you. One or the other of those worthies may be party to the plot but I don't think that both are. They don't care for one another enough for that. So neither one of them can hunt in the other's presence. In any event, they'll give you the rest of what you can carry and see you safely beyond the town. Go quietly and go quickly. And watch your back, boy, watch your back."

His uncle hesitated. For a moment Aurelius expected him to resume. But the king straightened and moved away through the dark, leaving his nephew holding a small doeskin bag and cord.

# Chapter Six

The afternoon sun was warm on his back. He had long since hit his stride for the day and his legs moved effortlessly while the thin mist of sweat coated his face and arms. Soon the chill of approaching twilight would begin to make itself felt but for now it was a fine spring day. Four full days on the trail had hardened his muscles and toughened his feet to his sandals. There had been no sign of pursuit and he was now well away from Oviedo. He did not really believe that either Ramiro or Nepotian had been party to the plot that had exiled him and no one else knew the direction or the time of his pre-dawn departure.

He was safe as far as danger from that quarter went. Of course there was always the chance of encountering bear, or boar, or wolf. But he was experienced in the woods. He was unlikely to happen upon them unaware. Renegade Astures were a more probable danger but his cousins had supplied him with a stout hunting bow, a double quiver of arrows, and his old hunting knife. So long as there was no ambush, so long as he encountered them singly rather than in a band, he could give a good account of himself—or so he thought.

The immediate problem was going to be food. The dried venison and the beans that Ramiro had given him were just about gone. The same steady walk that had set the tone of his body had also prompted his appetite and he had eaten perhaps a little more generously than was wise. If he had no other choice he could take the morning of the morrow and set some rabbit traps. Hares would be stringy after the long winter but they would also be hungry themselves and more active and a little more careless than they would be later in the season when they'd eaten more. Oro had a couple of extra bowstrings and the sinewy leather could be combined with the new, young saplings to furnish materials for traps. While he waited for a coney or two to spring his traps he could prospect for birds' eggs. It was a little early in the year for most of them but some of the more hardy fowl would have begun a new nest.

He had time to be patient since there had been no pursuit. The year was young and he was enjoying the fine weather and his own sense of well-being. He was a little lonely, especially at night after he had eaten, but his pride in his own independence compensated for that, in part anyway. The nightmare of his apprehension and near trial was receding. The image of Toda's father jerking and reeling as his throat had pumped blood was still vivid. He could recall Count Ordoño's face—cool and detached, merciless as a hawk's. Aurelius had seen bodies before, of course, but he had never seen a man actually killed. Animals yes, but a man was harder to forget. Had the old man been part of the plot? It was hard to believe that he didn't know his own daughter wasn't a virgin. He wondered how they had made the girl, Toda, agree to take a part. He wondered too, for a moment if she had begun to recover. What could she say?

It was a good feeling to know that his uncle believed in him. He was glad that he had not betrayed his cousins about their meeting in the woods. All the same, it made Oro sad that he had not been able to be open with his uncle. The whole business had been so confusing. He did not think that he had been the object of the scheme. He was the youngest of the possible heirs. Aurelius had half-persuaded himself that the trap was intended for Ramiro but the dark had misled the plotters to spring it on him instead. Did that mean that Nepotian was part of the conspiracy? His fat cousin had been the one who had suggested the meeting in the woods. That thought made the hair on the back of his neck stir and made him glad to be alone—at least for a while. So long as he was alone, on his own, life was simple. It was for his uncle, the king, to sort out the tangle and mete out justice to whoever was responsible. He himself was lucky, maybe, to be out of it.

But the present problem was food. Meat he could likely get without too much trouble. Birds' eggs too. Ramiro had also given him flint and steel so that he could smoke the one and roast the other at the cost of a little time. But his stomach would tell him soon enough that it wanted some filler too. Some half-rotten acorns for a starter and some of the mushrooms that were to be found now that the weather had warmed. Bread was out of the question but onions, some dried peppers, some tubers. It occurred to him that if he could locate a small village maybe there would be a smokehouse or a crib with turnips set off far enough from the house to make its plunder possible. His mouth watered at the prospect. He'd have to keep an ear open for hounds, of course. That sort of a find, with care, could furnish him supplies for a week and he wouldn't even lose the time that hunting for himself would take. When the theft was discovered he would already have six or eight hours lead and no one would try to follow him very far for a few vegetables and some dried meat.

So his musings had run. Then, a gift for sure, the young Asture hunter had chanced across his path. Oro shrunk back into the shadow of the trail but the other had never seen him. The hunter carried at his left side a young piglet whose throat dripped blood. Success, and maybe the lateness of the afternoon, had made the man careless. He looked to be about seventeen and he carried a light throwing-spear in his right hand. He had no shield but only the hunting knife at his belt. Clearly he was returning, pleased with himself, from a profitable hunt. His village could not be far off. It would be simple matter to follow him, spy out the village and its fields, and then wait for night and the going-down of the moon, to gather his provisions for a week.

Oro froze into a half-crouch. Ahead of him the hunter had just begun to cross a small clearing when two men emerged from the brush on its far side. Both had shields. One carried a club. The other's right hand held some sort of tangle of leather straps.

There was a crackling of undergrowth behind him. Oro instinctively prepared for the blow by pulling yet further into his crouch and so the club glanced from his quiver and caromed off the left rear of his skull. Oro shuddered under the impact, felt for purchase with his feet, and then the pain shot forward to his temples.

"Eeeeagh! Eeeeagh!"

The man was past him bounding towards the Asture youth. His right hand gripped a club, pierced and bound to his wrist with a hide thong. His left carried a circular shield.

"Run! Run! Run, you damn fool."

The words burst from Oro's lips without his even thinking. But the Asturian hunter did not stir. As will a deer sometimes, suddenly confronted by a wolf close-up, he froze even while he wheeled and perceived the closing of the trap. He did manage to set his spear but the burly assailant caught it at a slant on the surface of his shield and brushed it aside like a forest sapling. A second later he hurtled full speed into the body of the youth. The weight of his bulk and its impetus drove the other from his feet and the two crashed down in a tangle of limbs and shouting. The two other from the far edge of the clearing now ran to assist the third.

Slavers!

Aurelius was pounding back along the forest trail without taking concious thought. They would be after him in a minute. How long would it take the three of them to subdue the young Asture—bind him with those straps? After that, one of them would serve to herd him. The other two would be in pursuit of another prize. He himself!

He was running too fast. A misstep now and the hunt would be over. He could not afford to turn an ankle, to pull a muscle. The trail was too rough for this speed but he could not slow. The all-important thing now was to break visual contact. He must get far enough ahead of them so that they would have to track him rather than just to run him down. These first seconds were the crucial ones.

Then he was there! He rounded the bend in the trail that he had remembered even in his near panic. Oro slowed now to a fast trot. What direction? Where to leave the trail? To his left, the north, the country would gradually open and the chances increased that they could regain sight of him. To his right, the south, the cover was better and grew steadily more dense. But that land rose irregularly into the foothills of the mountains and this region was unknown to him. He could be run into a blind gorge and taken like the stupidest of cows.

To the south! The trail made his decision for him. A sudden bend and a deep thicket near its edge provided the cover he needed to leave it. He would leave small evidence of the direction in which he had gone. Another bend, not far ahead, would make it necessary for his pursuers to go at least so far before they could be sure that he had even left the trail. Perhaps there were yet other bends beyond that. He could not remember suddenly. He had been too careless, too secure, tracking the young hunter—not realizing that he too was being tracked.

No matter! The pursuit had surely begun. It was time! His mind had already instructed his muscles while he reviewed his course. Now he left the path in a long bound that carried him between two saplings into an area thick with ferns. Fortunately his luck held and there was no spur hidden below them to impale his legs .

He had landed still and balanced, from long practice at hunting. Slowly, deliberately, he began to retreat northwards backward through the fern. With his hands, he repaired most signs of his passage as he went. He could not do more. An experienced tracker would soon enough realize that his quarry had left the trail and would double back to sort out the spots where that could have been done. The best that he could expect was that he would gain a few minutes and that from now on they would have to track. So long as he was out of their sight he could set the pace. They would have to work on faint clues and whatever intuition they might possess from long experience of such hunts. If he could stay ahead of them till nightfall, he was safe.

The ringing was gone now from the blow on the head. There was an ache and that would grow as he ran but there was no help for that. Oro turned now and moved off with the steady lope of the forest-wise. His eyes searched out the ground before him for safe footing and maximum concealment of his passage. Alternatively, they sought out ease of progress and continuing cover ahead. He had recovered his breath now and ran easily. The late afternoon sun in the west scarcely touched his shoulders but gave him continuous bearings on his movement. He could not afford to be driven in circles.

* * *

They were good—very good—his trackers. The two of them had spread out behind him and he could faintly hear their halloos as they informed one another of their position and progress. They had lost him only briefly. He was being driven all right, driven towards the mountains. Aurelius had tried, earlier, to slant off towards the west but the sound of their calling had become much too close on that side. He could not afford to be sighted. He had veered south again and now the ground beneath him was rising perceptibly, both to his front and to either side as well.

He suspected that they knew as well that he had abandoned his attempt to cross their front. He could not go to earth for now they would be awaiting some such move. Good trackers that they were, they would be upon him in moments. Obviously they too were counting on the chance of a blind canyon. Please God they did not know the land!

Dusk was approaching now but he clearly was running a ravine. The sides were already impracticably steep. If he took to them he would been seen in minutes. His pursuers now knew as well that he could flee only in front of them. They had increased their pace and their halloos to one another were close enough to set the hairs of his neck to prickling. Any moment he expected to hear the cry that would announce that they had him in view. He was gradually increasing his own gait. The sweat on his shoulders was cold. He worried about his footing and fought off growing panic.

Of a sudden he saw it! His doom! Some ancient rockfall—landslide—had spread its bulk entirely across the ravine floor. The boulders were immense. The jumble of them rose forty, perhaps fifty, feet above the canyon bed. Given time he could have threaded them. Found a route to their beyond. But the slavers were too close. They would pick him off that wall like a beetle.

He had to make a stand now but he had little confidence in its success. They would be expecting that. His bow was good but light. Their shields could take the arrow and they would come on. He had no other weapons against their clubs except a knife, too short for that kind of work. Unless he got in a very lucky shot? Then too, he had never tried to kill a man before now. He was not sure that he could bring himself to it.

Then, just before his pursuers broke into view, he saw a possibility. Both sides of the ravine were sheer but on the left a tall pine had fallen against the cliff face. Instinctively he raced for it. There was no time to ensure that the tree was securely lodged. Rather, he threw himself on it, working his way upwards swiftly in the failing light. The shouts of the slavers rang out behind him. Up he worked, confident that they would not shoot him even if they had bows. The tree was steady. Its base must still be rooted! Twenty feet up it passed the lip of the rock and he was over.

Behind him the trunk was already beginning to shake with the ascent of the first of the slavers. Yet another ten feet he scrambled. There a litter of scree had stacked up against a number of larger boulders. With a strength born of desperation Oro hurled head-sized pieces just over the cliff's edge where the tree met it. He launched a virtual storm of projectiles and finally managed to break loose one of the larger boulders and send it rumbling down over the lip. He was rewarded with a string of expletives and then a shout.

Swiftly he knelt and notched an arrow, aiming barely a foot above the cliff's edge—but no one appeared.

They had retreated back down the tree for now. In the rapidly gathering dark they would have no time for another assault. Oro began to tremble with the release of tension. He felt light. As he unnocked the bow his own limbs threatened to betray him. Then, all at once, there was a sharp splat on the rock beside his head. What? A sling! They didn't have bows with them. He had not seen any. But they did have slings. At least one of them was very accurate with the weapon. He dropped alongside the boulder.

"Come down, boy. That could just have easily been your head. We don't want to kill you. Don't make us. Just come on down. We won't shoot."

The voice floated up from below, wheedling. The slaver knew his language. He was probably not an African but maybe a renegade Goth. Aurelius kept his cover. He didn't think that they could hit him in this light even if he stood up but he would take no chances. Neither did he reply. After a bit the voice started again.

"It will be best for you if you come down now, boy. It's going to get cold on the mountain pretty quick. We'll have a fire but you won't. We'll get you in the morning anyway. Come on down and have something to eat with us. We're not so bad. We're not cannibals, you know."

Still, Oro crouched by the boulder, not replying or even moving. They wouldn't try to come up now. He was almost positive. His would-be captor tried yet again.

"Last chance, boy. Think about it. We'll get you anyway. And it's a long walk to Córdoba. It can be mostly comfortable or it can be real hell. We can arrange it either way for you. We have other jackasses for our gear but you'll do just as well to pack it if we get really angry. Come down now, damn it."

But the young fugitive was up now. He could walk right up to the edge of the cliff and they could not see him. He could make them out from time to time. They were building a small fire a respectful distance away. They suspected that he might be desperate enough to launch an arrow or two in its direction. Before long he saw the third of their number come up with the hapless young Asture hunter bound and in tow.

Aurelius had no intention of loosing arrows futilely into the dark. He felt no such desperation at all. What the last of the light had told him was that a faint trail led up the cliff-face from this point. But it was distinct enough so that more than mountain goats had used it. So it led somewhere. Out of this ravine at least.

He would wait here till the moon had set. He had no desire for company or surprises. Then, when full dark returned, he would work his way up the trail and away. Come dawn, the slavers would have lashed some sort of saplings into rough ladders so that they could come at him all at once. But they would find that their bird had flown! He wished he could see their faces then.

# Chapter Seven

Killing the buck had been a mistake. At the time it had seemed so right—the natural thing to do. But since then everything had gone wrong.

The trail he had taken to elude the slavers had led him deep into the foothills of the Cantabrians. Going up in the dark had been touchy business. Coming down had been much more gradual but each step had taken him farther inland though the gradually broadening ravine into which he was descending seemed deserted.

At first it had worried him to depart so far from what he had conceived initially as a straight line west to Galicia. Then, as the bright sunlight started to clear the crests of the peaks ahead, he had begun to regain his sense of direction and then his composure. From what he remembered of hunters' tales at home, not too far ahead of him should be a pass through this northern spur and down into a river valley southwestward. The pass was no more than a mile high. Then if he ascended the river valley about three days journey there was another even lower that would lead him out of the mountains entirely and into Galicia not far east of the bishop's town at Lugo.

He was considering the possibility of that route as he descended the ravine that morning. The major problem was food. But that was going to be a problem in any event. Then too Oro still had a lively horror of the slavers. He had no idea how far they had spread their operations. It was early in the year for them to be ranging north of the Cantabrians. No one had sounded the alarm in Oviedo. For now, he was safer traveling into the mountains. The farther west he got the less likely he was to run into them again.

The lean-to decided it. He had come on it just before the ravine debouched into a larger valley. The small shelter was set back from the mouth of the ravine and a few paces within a grove of firs. From the opposite direction it would have been perfectly concealed until a traveler was directly parallel to it. Whoever had thrown it together on that site had obviously had that in mind. He had never anticipated anyone approaching from over the head of the ravine.

Aurelius waited and listened closely for a long time. Finally convinced that the builder was not in the vicinity he had approached the little shelter very, very gradually. There were animal tracks in the soft earth but none of them were very recent and none of them were of domestic animals. Whoever used the place was no shepherd. And he had no dog. He had left enough of his own footprints to make it obvious that he felt safe from detection here.

And he planned, whoever he was, to spend some little time here. There, in a corner of the lean-to, was a sack of rough material. When Oro opened it, gingerly, under a top blanket was a store of roots and a considerable quantity of dried meat. Quickly he had dumped about half of the foodstuffs onto the blanket and refolded it over them. The sack with the remainder of the food he threw over his shoulder and then he began to thread his way among the firs towards the mouth of the ravine. He felt acutely guilty. He had become a thief now! First a criminal, then an exile, now a thief! God knows, he would need the food. But he would not want to have to explain his plight to an enraged owner. And so he was creeping off, stealing away for sure!

But that feeling had lasted only until he reached the ravine's entrance and saw before him in the distance the steep climb towards the pass that he was seeking. Anyone who used that pass, in innocence, would long be visible to someone who stood regularly by the entrance to the ravine. They would be visible and vulnerable! Oro was suddenly sure that he understood the significance of the shelter. The man who had built it was himself an outlaw. This was to be his base of operations for the spring and summer. And the pass was to be his killing field. He would lay in wait here for the lightly armed, the solitary, the unsuspecting. After a summer of murder he would travel east to some village for the next winter. There he would present himself as a plunderer of Africans home from a successful season and would share some of his takings and enjoy the rest. He might, in fact, be a former soldier.

Doubly now, Aurelius had no wish to encounter the lean-to's owner. Careful about his own tracks, he began to work across the valley floor towards the pass. The bandit might be gathering wood in the hills. He might be looking for suitable materials for arrows. He might be hunting. Whatever was the case, Oro wanted a long start before he had to risk being sighted when he began the actual ascent into the pass on the other side.

As it had turned out, he had never even been pursued—so far as he could tell. His unwitting benefactor may have feared that he himself was being stalked. Whatever the case, the young man had climbed through the pass and descended, newly fed but still unscathed, into the river valley at the far foot of it. There he began to work his way upriver on the next leg of his journey.

It was by the river's bank a few days thereafter that he had come upon the buck. Or rather, it had come upon him. He had gone down to drink before commencing the day's travel. It had something the same in mind. But arriving later the animal had broken cover before it realized its danger.

Alerted by the sounds of motion that he sensed as much as heard, the young hunter had fitted an arrow to his bowstring. Then, seconds before it saw him, he saw the buck. He had only to release the bowstring and the shaft flew true and hard. The point plunged into the animal's side, missing the ribs and sinking most of its length into the deer's stomach. Stung and shocked, the buck leapt and half-turned, catching the shaft against a treetrunk and driving it further into his own vitals. Hurt yet again, the animal struggled for balance. Oro took the moment to loose another arrow and this time the shaft took the buck in the throat just above its joint with the chest.

Now the buck began to run for the shelter of the woods. Or rather, bound and leap towards the forest's edge. The hunter aimed yet again but the missle passed harmlessly over the shoulder of the fleeing animal. Aurelius himself was now on his feet and running. He had spent three of his precious arrows on this deer and he would not let it escape him. Just inside the forest cover, the buck crashed to its knees. The rear legs scrabbled desperately in the dirt as blood poured from the mouth. There was no longer any strength in its great forelegs.

The young hunter waited while the last throes of his prey gradually weakened and then ceased altogether. Only then did he approach. He jabbed it hard and frequently with a long, large branch—windfall from some distant storm—but the buck never stirred. Finally convinced that it was indeed dead, he approached and knelt before the head. He had killed his first deer! Dipping his hand in the blood around its mouth, he smeared some first on his forehead, then on his shoulders, and finally on his chest. The old hunters of his people advised that. They would have done it for him if he had been in their company when the kill was made. It drove the priests crazy. They said it was pagan idolatry and superstition! But the old men said that it brought luck!

Oro sat there on his haunches for some little time while his own blood cooled within him. He was a man for sure! It was only a little sad that Ram had not seen him do it. That Neppy had missed it! But it would make a great story. At least, it would make a great story if no one knew how lucky he had been. The buck had blundered into him. He had not had to stalk it. After that first shot, which had been good, the animal had virtually killed itself. How many good hunters were there in Oviedo, he wondered, and how many merely lucky ones? For that matter, how many good warriors were there? How many merely lucky ones?

In the course of his reflections, Oro gradually became aware that the ants had arrived, an army of them. They wound delicately around the dried blood to march into the mouth and the nostrils of the stricken deer. Damn! He straightened abruptly and hopped up and down in his sandals, killing scores and scattering the rest of them for the moment.

The carcass required his attention and with his knife he sliced open the belly and began to flense back the hide. He had seen this done before and had actually done it himself on smaller animals. But the buck was large and it seemed that the internal organs were masssive. With some difficulty, useless incisions, and a lot of ripping and sheer brute force, he finally had the animal cleaned. Taking it by the antlers, one of them broken from some past fight, he dragged the body free of the offal and down to the stream edge. There he dropped the head directly into the water. That would keep the ants away from the eyes anyway.

The efforts just expended caused him to consider for the first time what he would do with his kill. It was much too heavy to carry—all of it anyway. The head would have to be abandoned. It would quickly begin to rot in any event. If the ants wouldn't get the eyes, well, the crows would soon enough. From the body he might take the skin for a robe. For the rest, a haunch—perhaps one of the rear ones was best—would provide maximum meat and minimum weight. It would carry better too.

Aurelius set about the skinning of the buck. A proper butcher would have saved the hide from the legs, splitting them up for later use as ornamental quivers and much else, but he simply disregarded the extremities and cut around them, peeling the hide off the animal's trunk in one large, squarish piece. Then he rolled that into a bulky bundle and bound it with a spare bowstring. That done, he set about first skinning and then amputating one rear haunch. It was more difficult than he had anticipated. The smooth and powerful, striated muscles resisted manipulation and his knife had difficulties finding the joint for proper separation. Finally it was done but he was sweating and the day had worn on well towards noon.

Oro had relaxed for just a moment and when he saw the wolves. At the edge of the forest. There were two of them.

They sat like large, skinny dogs. But unlike dogs they were silent. They simply stared, unblinking, out of huge yellow eyes. Though it was between him and them and closer to them, the wolves ignored the offal of the buck. They respected his kill for now. There would be time for them to share it. Meanwhile they just watched him impassively.

After a minute or two, the young man rose slowly and collected his scanty gear. Careful to avoid sudden movements, he moved off upstream, along the water's edge. The skin, the haunch, and his food pouch could not be carried very easily and so he was forced to sling his bow and sheath his knife. The wolves just continued to sit and watch. He had expected them to do just that. When he had gone they would feed. First on the choicer bits of the stomach cavity, later on the muscle of the carcass. When they had finished, they would sleep in the sun. Later they would wake and feed again, perhaps sleep once more. Practical creatures, they had no interest in him either as food or prey so long as easier prospects presented themselves.

Through that day and the next he had packed that damned deer's leg joint. It was awkward to manage and beginning faintly to smell. By the evening of the second day he had decided to abandon it. He stripped some of the muscle tissue and hurled the rest of the leg far back into the woods. Over an open fire that night he attempted to smoke what he had kept. At home, the women would have soaked the meat for days before even attempting this. Deer were active animals! Oro did little more than burn the outside of the pieces. He could have done better if he'd allowed a good bed of coals to build up. But that would have meant either using up a good part of one day or letting a fire burn far into the night. If anyone were to pass nearby, a fire of that size and duration would make its kindler an easy target for some kind of mischief. As it was, chewing the half-cooked meat gave him almost as much exercise as the walking he did while he tried to eat it. But he could suck the juices, soften it in his mouth, swallow bits and pieces, and then spit the indigestible parts out.

The hide gave him as much trouble. After he had selected a place to camp at night, he unrolled it and cleaned the fleshy side more thoroughly. The bits of fat and muscle remaining were fast rotting and the whole thing stunk. He scraped and scraped and threw the little piles of mortified flesh that accumulated far back into the woods, away from his campsite. But the smell continued and the thing got stiffer and stiffer. He tried peeing on it and then beating it with a flat stone. That was what he'd seen the women of the hunters do at home. They had little boys or girls pee on the skins and then they worked it in.

But gradually he came to the conclusion that the women must have been doing something else as well. The hide didn't get any softer. It sure didn't smell any better. Carrying it was becoming a bigger nuisance every day. What the hell! Abruptly, and in a foul mood anyway, he threw it too away late one morning, and went on without it. It had been a waste. The whole business had been a waste. He had killed the buck for nothing. A few lousy scraps of meat that made his jaws hurt when he tried to eat them was all that he had left. He wouldn't tell this part of the story when he went home. If he went home?

Oro had begun to get very lonely, homesick, even before the rains began. But they didn't help. He knew this type of rain. It could be just like this at home. The days were uniformly gray. Neither at daybreak nor in the evening did he get more than a glimpse of a little bit of sickly sunshine. When he should have had full sun warming his back and shoulders at midday there was only dank gray mist, coating his hair and body, seeping through his clothes.

Luckily it was spring but at this elevation it got cold

enough once the rain hit. Damn. Spells like this at home you retreated to the house fire and resisted the best efforts of anyone to get you to leave it. You sat around and listened to the stories of the old men. They told you how to beat the Africans, how to enjoy their women, or how to track a bear to find honey. What was the quickest way to climb a tree in case the bear discovered you! In between stories you flattered them and tried to wheedle a bit of cider or wine out of them. Mostly it was still miserable until the sun came back but you got a little heat anyway and a dry place to sleep if you were attentive.

Here, in the mountains of Galicia, Oro had gradually become wet through and through. It wasn't just his clothes, he thought. No, the water had crept into his flesh. He was all puckered and gray himself. There wasn't any dry place to sleep. After the first few days the rain had penetrated the tree cover overhead. It soaked into the winter's decay on the forest floor so that walking in it was almost like walking on the floor of a pond. The stuff stuck and it chilled. At night there were no dry leaves to be had. Oro cut small fir branches with his knife to pile on top of the crap but they were not much drier themselves by this time. Lying between the thatch of his lean-to and the bed of firs, he tried to avoid the very worst of the rain and cold but the mist and the damp crept around the make-shift roof and seeped up through the fir branches. He shivered and slept miserably. Even devising new and more obscene ways to curse his plight palled after a time.

He knew the ways that a hunter was supposed to deal with life in the forest. He had heard them all. But where in the hell was the cave that was supposed to offer shelter? He had seen a few but they had been shallow with wet floors and he had gone on in expectation of finding better. Now he had no idea where they had been even! The worst part of it was that he had been without a fire for three days. He had his flint and steel. He had his little pouch of tinder. But by now it was so wet that he was not able to get it to catch most of the time. And if he did, the little twigs that he had gathered and split were so green or so thoroughly soaked themselves that he had to put his tinder out so as to save it. He couldn't get a starter fire sufficient to thaw out anything to the point that it would burn on its own. He had to save some of his tinder!

If he just pushed on, sooner or later he might get out—he might get beyond this weather. He needed to get out of the mountains. The wind sliced through his wet tunic, mocking the thought of sun and warmth. Only his throat was dry, scratchy. It had been that way since he woke in the morning. It would be difficult to swallow but the fact was that he was out of food. He should try to hunt or to trap something. Even if he couldn't cook it without a fire he could drink some of the blood. He needed the strength. He was getting a little shaky. His legs didn't have the feeling that they should have. But his bowstrings were wet through! For now they were useless.

Dully he told himself that he needed to keep an eye out for birds' nests. Two or three eggs would take the edge off the empty feeling in his stomach that was beginning to make him nauseous. But the rain and mist made visiblity poor in the forest and the thought of shinnying up a tree made him wearier still. Maybe it was best just to push on. The light was beginning to fail. He needed a drier place to sleep more than he needed food anyway. Perhaps at the bottom of this hill there would be an uninhabited cave with a dry floor. Maybe even some old, dry debris on its floor to bury himself in! Or dry branches that would burn!

Insensibly Oro increased his pace a little. He was descending an old road, a Roman road. No one built them like the ancients. This one he had been following since the afternoon before. He had stumbled on it and knew at once that it led somewhere. At the end of it there would be a town or at least a village. It might snake down one side of the hill and then up the other but it was going somewhere—he was going somewhere! He was no longer lost!

If he just slogged along it far enough he would find people, houses. Besides, the Romans had sometimes built stone way- stations, huts, along their roads. Before night he might chance on one of those that had something like half a roof left anyway. The old Romans had built solidly. Their stonework lasted forever. Like the stones of this road. They were uneven maybe, from the frosts of four or five hundred years, but they were still easy under the feet. Almost smooth!

He was sliding! His rotten sandals suddenly could get no purchase on the wet moss covering the stones of the roadway. Oro tried to regain his balance but his legs would not respond properly. He felt for a grip but the quick, irregular motion had unsettled his sense of place; he felt that he was falling even before he actually began to fall. His frantic exertions only made his disorientation worse. Far away, he felt his head strike the stones. It didn't hurt that much. Hardly at all actually. He could just relax and let himself slide on the wet stone paving. You got really hurt when you tensed! They always told you to relax. He'd come up against something. Something would stop him. Then he'd be all right. Just don't get tense. Don't break anything.

* * *

His head ached! He was laying in some kind of a small ditch. It had water in the bottom. That was bad. He should get out of it. His legs seemed to be okay. If he could just get them underneath him. It was slippery in the damn ditch. He was tired. There wasn't enough light left to see where he could find something to brace against, to pull on. Have I been asleep? God, I'm cold. How long have I lain here? This could be the end of me!

His head spun. He scrabbled frantically in the slimy mud, finding nothing solid. He must wait a moment. He mustn't panic. Panic was the enemy in the woods. Stop and take a deep breath. Just wait a minute. Get your wind back. Take the time you need. The old hunters always said to....

The black was everywhere. Aurelius slid into it. It was restful. The agitation ceased and the waters of the ditch subsided, rested gently against his body.

# Chapter Eight

He was hot—suffocating! The sweat was running off him in great rivulets. He could feel the flush of his face and the pounding in his head. A great soft weight pressed down on him. It enveloped him. His breath came in short pants. Whorls of colored light spun dizzily. He pressed on his eyelids but they were still there. They flexed and danced. They flashed close by and then receded.

And always he was wrapped around in a soft, yielding mass. He fought against it. He would smother! He could feel the hair. It was his buck's skin! He was trapped inside the skin of the deer he had killed! Someone had sewn him into it. The skin was like a tunic but it was too hot. With his arms he tried to strip it from his body but the fit was too good. There must be stitching somewhere. If he could find it—but the hair was long. He couldn't find the stitches for the hair of the pelt. He would never get it off.

But the skin wasn't empty! It was full! Every way he twisted a soft, wet mass lay against his body. He could feel his own sweat running into it. And its fluids were running into him! The offal! Whoever had made the deerskin tunic for him had forgotten it! They had not cleaned it! He was sewn into an uncleaned carcass. He could feel the heart beating alongside his own! Oro could feel the pumping of the lungs of the buck and the flux and reflux of its bowels. He was afraid. He was terribly afraid.

He tried to put his hands up. He wanted to put his hands up to his head. He wanted to be sure that he did not have antlers. He wanted to be certain that they had taken the horns off. If the horns were growing out of his head he could never go home again. Ram would laugh at him.

He must know if he had grown antlers! But he couldn't get his arms free. The women had sewn his arms inside the pelt. His arms had been free a moment ago. They had come back while he slept and had sewn his arms inside. The buck's heart was still beating. He could feel it. He was going to scream. He tried to choke it back. Warriors didn't scream. But he could hear it echoing. It came out of his mouth and he was unable to stop it.

The slavers were all screaming too. They were shouting at him to stop but they were screaming too. The noise hurt his head. He pressed his hands against his temples to stop the pain. He pressed harder and harder until something broke inside his skull—and the pain all melted and ran down inside. He felt it in the back of his throat. Then it made a nausea in his stomach. Now the liquid pain was running out his bowels. It was going away and it would leave him all empty. He was empty and weak. Weak and filthy! The pain was going. It was very far off. He could hardly feel it. The heat was draining out of him with it.

If only the forest weren't so cold! The snow kept falling -kept piling up. He would have to find some firewood soon. His light tunic just wasn't going to protect him much longer. By now he could scarcely make out the outlines of the lean-to. It was almost covered with the snow. If he hadn't helped Ram and Neppy to build it he wouldn't have been able to find it. But he knew where it was. He just had to get inside to keep warm.

"Hello, Aurelius."

It was Toda. She had found the lean-to in the forest. She was all right—she had gotten her senses back.

"Come in, Aurelius. Come in and stay with me."

She wasn't angry with him anymore. She would tell the king that he had never raped her. Then he could go home. He could come out of the forest and live in the palace again. It was all going to be all right again. It was just that it was so cold!

But Toda didn't mind the cold. She was smiling. She was holding out her arms to him.

"Come on in, Oro. It's too late to be hunting. Come into the lean-to and play with me. My father went out. He'll never know."

Toda didn't seem to mind the cold. But she was naked! He tried not to look at her because he didn't want her to see him looking at her. Not when she was naked. Girls got angry when you tried to do that.

"Help me, Oro. I don't understand what they're doing. But you understand. You have to help me. I'm only a girl."

The voice seemed far away now but Toda was right there. She stood naked with her arms still outstretched to him. He didn't want to look at her but it seemed rude to ignore her pleas. And she grew as he did. That is, her breasts grew. As he stared now, horrified, they swelled to the size of gourds, to the size of melons, beyond ...!

She knew too! She had seen him staring at her! Toda tried now to support her breasts with her hands but they were too small. That great, soft weight spilled around and over her palms and down already to her navel. Their mass was pressing her down and down into the snow. She was disappearing into the snow, sinking little by little.

"Please, Aurelius, please! They are pushing me down! They will kill me!"

But Toda was gone. She had sunk into the snow, breasts and all. He reached for her but all that he could feel was the wet. It was gone. Toda had melted the snow. Or she had melted with the snow. All that was left was a warm mist that floated up around him. He could feel it warming him. It enveloped him. It rubbed against him.

Toda was coming back! The girl was coming back to him in the mist. He could see her. No! It was Neppy! His cousin was coming to rescue him—to lead him out of the forest and back to their uncle. He knew that it was Neppy. He had that absurd round and white belly. He never did enough, ran enough, hunted enough. He was going to be really fat before very long. But I musn't kid him about it. He'll be angry if I do.

"You shouldn't have killed her, Oro. She was just a girl. She didn't know anything."

"I didn't kill her, Neppy. She just disappeared. She melted. Toda was just here and she could talk."

"You let them kill her. You wouldn't talk. You wouldn't tell. You let her melt. I would never have sent her to you if I had thought that you would let her melt. I thought that she would be good for you. That she'd be your first woman. But you let her slip and fall. And that makes it my fault—but you were the one that wouldn't talk."

Neppy was really angry with him now. He was shaking. He had taken the knife from behind his back. It was the poinard! It was Count Ordoño's poinard! Behind Neppy Toda's father was signing to him to run. The old man stood there with the great gash in his throat and motioned to Oro frantically.

"Run! Run like you did from the slavers!" The words echoed in the air. They came from the hole in his throat. His mouth was closed!

Aurelius tried to run. His legs wouldn't move. He attempted wildly to move but the ground caught his feet. Neppy kept getting closer. Oro could see the point of the knife. It dripped blood. He seized a tree branch and pulled himself backward. He pulled himself away from that bloody point.

"I protected you, Neppy. I protected you and Ram. I didn't tell. Uncle would have been angry. He would have had us all whipped. It was treason, you know. It really was."

"No. Ram built the lean-to. He had the girl there. He was going to rape her but I made him leave her for you. Ram had lots of girls but you and I didn't have any. I sent her to you and you spoiled it. You killed her."

"That's not the way it was, Neppy. You didn't know anything about it. The girl wasn't in the lean-to. Toda was in the hut waiting for her father."

"I know everything about it. And you can't tell uncle. You killed the girl and now you're trying to kill me. You'll tell Ram and then he'll beat me up again.

Nepotian wasn't listening. He was advancing, advancing, with the poinard glistening in the sunlight. Oro's feet were caught in the muck. They each weighed more than his entire body. He had to struggle to lift first one and then the other.

Nepotian's eyes had turned black. His nose grew longer. It was turning into a beak! The feathers of his head were sprouting down along his neck!

"Please, Neppy, we played together! We always shared everything! We'll go look for Toda together."

"Eeeaaw! Eeeaaw!"

The hawk lunged forward, the dagger still at ready. It was leveled at his stomach.

Aurelius stumbled backward. He was at the cliff edge. The ground was going under his feet. He could feel it slip. His arms grasped wildly but there was no purchase. There was nothing but air! He was falling into the canyon. He was floating down, down, down. Above him the hawk launched into the blue and began to descend on him in wide, lazy circles.

* * *

Just when the fever broke was hard to know. The delirium over, he was weak. He lay there under the skins watching the charcoal burner. The man was short and dark. Every pore and line of his body appeared to be filled with the black soot that was the mark of his livelihood. It coated the hairs of his nostrils and floated from his scalp when he shook his head in puzzlement. He moved about the hut like a huge, animated charred hunk, silent, not speaking more than the necessary word or two of direction.

But he had found Aurelius in the ditch beside the road and had carried him home. He and his wife had dried him and put him into their own bedding by the fire. They had warmed him between their own bodies and had restrained him in his deliriums. Now that the fever had left him the woman spooned soups into him and forced porridges down him. His strength was coming back.

She spoke as rarely as the man. "Eat. Sleep now." Even then it sufficed to make the man frown and mutter. He seemed to think that she was chattering unnecessarily. Between the two of them the daily routine passed almost without communication. Long ago, perhaps, they had established their simple wants. Now words had become superfluous.

The woman was yet shorter and more squat than her husband. She was a boulder of a woman moving on legs that bulged with muscle. Her arms were greater in girth than were Oro's thighs. Her breasts hung, pendulous, like gourds, like melons whose weight the vine could no longer tolerate and was about to let drop. Her face was almost perfectly circular and her small, dark eyes seemed to disappear into the creases of flesh. Her nose was flat and broad and overhung a great wide slab of a mouth. Altogether she was an extraordinarily ugly woman. Old too, Oro thought. Probably already thirty-five.

His own mother had died in the giving of birth to him. As a result, almost from the time that the wetnurse had pushed him away, Aurelius had run free. The women of the palace had seen to his rudimentary needs but he had formed little personal relationship with them or they with him. Consequently, he had largely ignored them as adults of even less significance than the males. He had lived in a world of children and of his cousins, Ram and Neppy. Now he supposed that this woman was like all old women but, actually, he had virtually no memories of others with whom to compare her.

In the morning the man left for his forest ovens early, before the sun had begun to overtop the trees at the edge of the clearing. He moved in a gray half-light that paled even more at the prospect of trying to illuminate his animated darkness. The forest in its turn opened to swallow him. He made no sound as he departed and the morning noises of the forest were neither diminished nor increased by his leaving.

I will get up this morning, Oro thought. I have my strength back. I wonder where I am? In a little while I will get up.

The woman was alongside of him in the bedding. She did not rise with the man. She never did. There was no need. Aurelius was vaguely uncomfortable with the smell of her body, with the full rasp of her snore. It was familiar already—still.... Perhaps I will get up.

But the woman had ceased to snore. The bulk of her body lurched, pressing against him. She was wet with the warm, morning dampness. The hair on the back of his neck rose in fright. The woman had taken his genitals in her enormous hand and was caressing them softly. He could hear her guttural murmur.

"Sweet boy. Dear boy. Lay still now. I won't hurt you. Let me make you well. Let me make you happy."

He could hear her panting. She was sweating now for sure and it dripped down on him. One of her legs, like a tree trunk, lay across his own. With horror he felt himself beginning to respond to her massage. He was stiffening.

"Wait! Wait a minute! I'm not ready. I have to pee."

"No you don't, darling boy. That can wait. It will be all right. Wait and see."

"No. I can't. I can't wait. Give me a minute. I'll only be a minute. Then I'll be all right."

Slowly, reluctantly, the woman moved back and released him. From those tiny little, recessed eyes she peered at him all questions. The panting subsided and she filled her lungs. Her entire body swelled with the intake.

"Do it then. Do it quickly just out there. No tricks now. And then come back to Guntroda, sweet boy. Come back to Guntroda and after I'll make you a fine breakfast, a fine porridge. You'll like that. You'll like all of it."

The woman smiled now and her great mouth gaped. Her fetid breath poured out and over him. He almost gagged.

Aurelius rose slowly and turned towards the door of the little hut. To the right, on a the nub of a limb projecting from one of the uprights that braced the wattle wall, hung his tunic, his empty food sack, his bow and knife. Now he darted to them. Stripped them with one reach from the peg.

"Don't!"

With all her bulk the woman was half up already as she divined his intent. The vast expanse of her naked body hove up from the bedding. Her rounded features were contorted and something like fright made her look as if she were about to weep.

"Stop, boy. Don't run off. You owe me! I saved your life. Is it too much to ask? Just a little pleasure. You won't miss it. Then you can go if you want to. Just a little caress for old Guntroda to remember from her sweet little boy. That's all I want. I swear it."

The woman was up now. Absurdly threatening in her vast size and her ludricrous nudity. Oro clutched his few possessions in front of him. Now he dragged his knife from its sheath and held it out towards her. He swept it back and forth only inches from those swaying breasts.

"Get away! Get away!. If you don't get back I'll cut you. If you come near me I'll kill you. I really will. I mean it."

The woman stood. Her face slowly registered a mix of shock and confusion. She was not sure that he would stab her. He might. But she was terrified that he would leave. A great tear broke from one eye and then was followed by a torrent of water from both. A strange, primitive sound broke from her lips, her entire body shuddered. She began to cry, to sob. Her mouth twitched but no other sound issued from it. Only the sobs. As she did, she pressed forward a little. It was only a pace or two but it sufficed to bring her within the arc of his blade. A fine line of blood started across the forward-protruding expanse of those breasts.

Aurelius stared unbelieving, gasped himself, and then seized on her confusion, on the chaos of the other's pain, realization, emotion. He edged towards the doorway of the hut. Suddenly he was free. He was out the door. Turning he ran, reeling a little with weakness, but swift for all of that. He ran with gradually accelerating bounds and leaps. Behind him he could hear the pursuing voice of his benefactress.

"Stop, you little bastard! Don't you run away. You were dead and half-frozen when my man picked you up. I warmed you with my body then. I gave you your life back. You owe me! I only want a little love from you."

Oro ran on. Only her words pursued him but that was enough.

"God damn you, stop! You didn't run from Guntroda then. You clung to this body. You burrowed into it like a bear cub. You took all the warmth I had to give you then. Now you wrinkle your nose and run but then you couldn't get enough of me. You owe me, you little shit! Stop! Stop, please?"

But he ran. He ran until the stabbing in his side threatened to break entirely out of his skin. He was not sure where he was in the forest but he heard no pursuit. The old woman couldn't catch him and the old man wouldn't care. He hadn't taken anything of his.

Aurelius would have run further but his head was beginning to reel. His empty stomach had begun to heave. He stopped, leaning against a broad tree trunk. He set his back to it. Slowly, his breath began to come back. He thought of what had just happened and he shivered. He squeezed his eyes together but he could see yet the inside of the hut, the bedding, the woman. His whole face quivered. For a moment he thought that he was going to cry.

Then he began to laugh. He began to laugh and his entire body started to shake with the tremors. He laughed and the power went out of his legs. Slowly, he slid back down the tree until he was resting on the ground itself. His eyes watered. He lost his breath again. Still he laughed—hysterically almost—finally weakly, subsiding but with renewed spasms of laughter now and again.

After a time, he rose and donned his tunic. He swung up his bow and food sack, hung his knife at his waist. Sun at his back, he took up his journey once again. It was more than two hours later when it occurred to him that he no longer had his uncle's ring!

# Chapter Nine

The village lolled in the late afternoon sun. Little children pursued one another around the wattle huts, dodging behind harried mothers busy at the grinding of corn. Maternal shouts and threats followed them but they paid no heed. This was their season. Time to chase. Time to push. Time to fall breathless in a heap. Their laughter rose with the thin smoke of damped fires to give meaning and content to the sun-washed air.

Now and then the village women themselves looked up, wiped the beads of sweat from their foreheads, smiled a little, and shook their tresses. They remembered. Their time was gone but they remembered the sweetness. One or another of them shifted, let the blood flow again in calves and feet, and returned to the querns. The querns never really stopped. One had to eat. Meal made bread. Meal made porridge. Meal made dumplings. The little ones ran and jumped but the more they did the sooner they would come back—bellies empty—whining for food. Men made grain but women made meal.

The men, however, were idle just now. Sometimes it seemed that they were always idle. The time between the sowing of the grain and the reaping of it went on forever in the sun of summer. In this place or that the men sought refuge from the children. They sought refuge from their wives. They bound themselves up in small male knots with their friends and made jokes that weren't very funny and told the stories that every one of them had heard a hundred times. Their lies, their boasts filled out the lazy time until they too would decide that they were hungry and would come, complaining like the very children, seeking food to still their mouths.

But just now they were busy. Just now they had a new thing! The boy, he wasn't much more than that, had come up from the holy man's hut out at the verge of the forest. Three days he had been there. All the women of the village had crept round to peek at him from a safe distance. But he had never come up to the village before. He was well favored. A little scrawny maybe but strong-limbed. Good brown eyes. A tousled mop of thick, black hair. Tanned and tall he was. The old ladies sighed. The girls would bear watching with this new one about. Perhaps more than just the girls at that.For now the men had him. Later the women would learn what they had found out.

Miro, the headman, was the one to question him, of course. It was part of being leader. He had the dignity that the loss of one leg and the onset of age can give. He was not an ordinary man. Not many give their leg to a bull and fight their way back to survival. Two of his mostly-grown sons hung on the outskirts of the little crowd of men. He had not, Miro often jested, lost the best of his legs to the bull.

"You stay with the crazy man, boy? Are you going to stay with that looney old shepherd?"

"He took me in," replied Aurelius, "for now he gives me shelter and a little food. I don't know anyone else here."

Miro frowned. "He gives you food that he wouldn't have if our women didn't take pity on him. He doesn't do a damn thing. He just sits there and stares and talks to himself. He's just eating, breathing, mumbling bad luck as far as we can see. One of these days we're going to go down there and burn the hut, kill him."

One or two of the men in the group nodded in agreement. Others just stared at Oro to see what he would say. Aurelius did not know what he should say. It was not a friendly group. He spoke quickly, out of nervousness.

"You say that he once was a shepherd? Of your village?"

"Yes, of our village. He used to run our sheep and some of his own up in the hills. Then one fine day he just left them. Just walked off and left them, he did. A good thing that the wolves weren't out in force. We'd have lost the whole lot, not just the few we did lose. Then he built himself that little hut you've seen on the edge of the forest and he's been sitting there ever since. All he ever does is make our wives have crazy dreams and eat the food that they take down to him."

Miro obviously liked to talk. He enjoyed being the center of attention. Oro thought that it would be a good idea to lead him to talk some more.

"You say that he just walked off and began to live by himself? Why did he do that? Did he ever say why?"

"How do we know, boy? He just went crazy up there in the hills alone with nobody but the sheep to talk to. Maybe he got too friendly with them. You've heard the old definition of 'virgin wool' haven't you, boy? A sheep that can run faster than his shepherd."

Some of the men in the crowd chortled, shuffled. One of them spoke.

"If that would do it, Miro, there wouldn't be a sane shepherd in the whole world. They're all weird to begin with. That's why they become shepherds in the first place."

Others in the group laughed shortly at this sally. Miro

glared at the offender. It was his place to make the jokes. To keep the lead he continued.

"Some of us were mad as hell at him, boy. You can imagine. Five or six perfectly good sheep dead. We questioned him allright. We beat the hell out of him. But all he ever told us was that God had called him to sit over there. Not to do anything, you understand. Just to sit over there and wait. We asked him why and he said he didn't know why. He said that sooner or later God might tell him why and that, then again, he might not. We beat him till he bled but that's all we could get out of him.

"And he's been sitting there ever since. Doesn't get up to go anywhere or to do anything except to go shit once in a while. Sits there and mumbles to himself or just stares into thin air. But that's enough to convince the women that he's a holy man. Most of the women in the village think that he talks to God. They take him food and ask him questions sometimes but he never answers them. He ignores the lot of them. And still the silly old cows think that he's some kind of a saint even though he smells more like a pig and looks like a scarecrow.

"So they take him food and the result is that he stays here instead of wandering off to die somewhere else. He'll bring a curse on us all yet. We should have killed him at the beginning. We will yet."

This last sounded to Oro as if the old headman was trying to work up nerve to do just that. Miro's hand tightened on the crutch that he used to half-support himself. With those biceps and those heavy, muscled hands he could crack the little hermit like an acorn if he once decided to do it. Then the chief turned away from that thought which perhaps he did not wish to come too close to resolving finally at just this moment.

"But now you're here, boy. And you're eating our food too. Or you will so long as that nut puts up with you. And that's a little strange too. Why should he take you in? You don't know him? He doesn't know you? Who in the hell are you, anyway? Where do you come from? What do you want here?"

Aurelius knew that he had to be careful now. No one liked strangers to begin with. And he had happened to meet the outcast of the whole community first. There was a feeling of something ugly in the afternoon air suddenly. Their first impulse was to hate him. He had started off all wrong.

"I don't know why he took me in. He was the first person I came across when I got here. I never knew him before. He didn't know me."

Miro eyed him sourly. "Friends right off, huh? Never met before? Funny business, boy. You sleep with him? He use you now instead of his sheep friends? Do you like being a holy man's whore?"

The young man was taken back by the directness and the savagery of the attack. Now there was real danger. The group of men had gotten immobile. There was a stiffness and a tension to it.

"Its not that.... He had just been kind to me. Nothing more. I don't know why. He just is. He's being kind to a stranger."

Miro pressed on. His temper was up. Maybe it would be a good thing to bloody this pretty boy. It would be a lesson to the women who hung around trying to listen. It would be a lesson to the old crazyman besides. The headman was, despite himself, a little in awe of the former shepherd but this boy was another matter. He balanced his weight more securely on his remaining leg. His heavy crutch was free now. His hand moved it idly in the dust. The men stirred. They had seen this manuever before and knew what it portended. There might be some fun in the making—some little excitement for the afternoon.

Oro saw the chief's movement too and understood them as well. He could evade the crutch easily enough but then the whole crowd would be on him. His own blood was racing now.

"Who are you, boy? Where do you come from? Why do you come here? What are you looking for anyway?"

The questions did not look to an answer. They were the spring for the trap. His answer, no matter what it was, would trip it.

"I come from Oviedo of Asturias. I come looking for Count Muño."

The completely unexpected quality of the reply won some time. The hesitation of the headman was visible. He had not counted on such a thing. Miro's brain spun dizzily. The men watched, waiting for him to crush this lad. But he was not too sure now. Maybe the boy had not made it up. He blustered.

"Our count? You came to see our count and you begin by taking up with an old wildman? Who are you to have business with Count Muño?"

"I am a cousin of his. I have been sent from Oviedo with a message for him. On the trip I became sick and I am just now recovering but I have come here to seek him out."

Miro let his weight settle back on his crutch. This was embarrassing. Worse, it could be dangerous. What if the young fool were indeed a cousin of the count. He could lose his head for the way he had threatened him already. The count had a notoriously short temper. Safety lay in being stupid. The story was not likely. On the other hand, it was quick—bright—if it had been invented. If it proved untrue, well, the boy's destruction by the count would be entertaining and he wouldn't be involved. It could be fatal to the old man as well.

"You come here without attendants, without a horse, without food, and almost without clothes on your back, and you expect poor honest farmers to recognize you and hail you as a gentleman? Where is your proof, young man? If you are what you say, we would welcome you into our homes, of course. But how are we to be sure that you are what you say?"

This last had almost the tenor of a whine about it and Aurelius pressed the advantage.

"My business is with the count. I don't explain it to farmers. When I find him the count himself will be proof enough of what I claim."

Miro had the uneasy feeling that this young man was telling the simple truth. Strange as it was he told his story with calm and simplicity. He didn't seem to feel the need to hide anything or to invent anything. And he certainly didn't have the look of a farmer's whelp about him. The headman's mind turned furiously. After all, he had some experience of the wider world in his youth. If the boy was what he claimed to be then no one would thank him for meddling in the affairs of the great. And if he was not, then the youth had already probably forfeited his own life. All that remained for him to do was to salvage his own prestige.

"You don't have to find the count, young man. He's been on a hunt in the east for some few days now but he will return. Then he will be interested to see his new relative from Oviedo. You may be sure that he will call on you as soon as he learns of your visit to our part of the world. He has a palace not far from here but I wouldn't advise you to go there before he returns. His bailiffs might not treat you as gently as we have. Especially since you have no proof of who you say that you are.

"For now, maybe you should just continue as you have so far. We're friendly folk, here. Just try not to involve us in your business. It is no affair of ours. We're simple farmers and we don't want any trouble with anyone."

Aurelius knew this tack and this tone. He'd seen people take it with his uncle when they came to realize that they had overreached themselves. It gave him a little thrill of power. At the same time he recognized the good sense of what the old man had said. Without the king's ring on his finger the caretakers of the count's estate would probably think themselves prudent to hold him prisoner until their master's return. That much at least. If the politics were particularly touchy here, some one of them might even think it better advised if he had an accident. They could easily explain a sound beating as a remedy for his impudent presumption. If it went too far, well, these kinds of things happen out of an excess of zeal.

"I think that you are right, father. I never meant anyone any trouble here and the simplest thing for me to do, while I'm waiting for the return of my cousin, is to continue as I have been. I appreciate your hospitality and will reward it."

Best to give the village headman a sop. He had to retain his dignity or he would become even more dangerous. He had no power to help Oro now but he did have considerable opportunity to cause mischief if he regained his nerve. Let them all think that there was better chance of eventual gain in acting graciously for now at least.

Miro watched and barely concealed his frustration as the youth turned and walked off. That son-of-a-bitch was patronizing him! Well, the great ones did that without thinking. But he'd better be what he said he was. Otherwise,

I'll spit on his bones when the count is through with him. For now he could be content with a brand new story for the old lady. God, they did like a bit of news. It was even enough to stop their mouths for a little while. He was beginning to feel hungry.

Aurelius walked off with what he hoped was the requisite dignity. He needed to strike just the right note. These people were still dangerous. He had to appear confident although he felt far from it. When he reached the old shepherd's hut, Alvitus was seated just exactly where he had been when the youth had left a couple of hours earlier. Oro would have looked to see if he were covered with dust if the day had not been so still. The way he sat, crosslegged, looking towards the forest's interior, hour after hour in the daytime and well into the night. You expected to touch him and see him fall over. He could be dead except for the fact that he sometimes chanted. Oro was sure it was Latin, church Latin. You would think that his legs would be withered, the way he sits.

But he does eat. Not much, but he eats. Cold food! When was the last time that he had a fire? It was all right now that the summer was almost here, but what does he do in winter? The youth thought of his own recent illness and shuddered despite himself. No use asking that kind of idle question for the old man would not answer it. Oro knew that already. Alvitus would answer him if he thought the question deserved it. He did speak to Aurelius even if he didn't to the village women and if the village men didn't speak to him.

"The men in the village hate you, Alvitus. Do you know that? They have never forgiven you for losing some of their sheep. They resent their women feeding you too. For now they are afraid to stop the women but they'll do you harm sooner or later. I could hear it in their voices."

The little man didn't stir. He didn't turn to face Oro. He probably had been heavy once. One could see that his bones were big where the skin stretched over them. That skin was now the color of old leather. On his head he boasted only a few long strands of jet black hair. His hands and feet were absurdly large. They seemed in danger of falling off, restrained solely by his total lack of motion. Even his chest did not move with his breathing. More than once in the past few days Oro had had the giddy expectation that when the other did move his parts would separate, like the limbs of the clay dolls that little girls made when they had sat too long in the sun.

"They don't hate me for a few miserable sheep, young man. They hate me because I once was a shepherd and now I am a holy man. They hate me because now I'm a holy man and they are still peasants. But they will not kill me. Nor you either. You don't have to fret about it. They won't kill me unless God deserts me. But God won't desert me if I don't desert Him and I have no intention of doing that."

All of this was said in a perfectly matter-of-fact tone and the little man did not even raise his voice. He could scarce be heard. Yet his words sent a thrill along Oro's spine.

"You told the villagers that God called you. What does He want you to do?"

"I don't know. He did not tell me. Just to come here and wait. Nothing more."

"Does God speak to you now? Is He with you now?" Aurelius was uncomfortable giving voice to the questions. They sounded silly to him. If he had spoken so to one of the palace priests back at Oviedo they would have had him whipped for impertinence, or maybe for sacrilege.

"No, He has not spoken to me since that first call. And He is not with me. He has never been with me. But He is there, over there somewhere—somewhere in the forest—brooding in the forest. I can feel a presence that abides in that dark place. So I am waiting here as He commanded and until a new command is uttered."

"But you could die here. You would die if the women of the village did not feed you. How can you know that it was not a dream? How can you be sure that it was not the devil who spoke to you? In the village they think you mad."

"It is not for those idiots in the village to judge. They understand nothing about the ways of God. Nor do you, young man. Do you think it is an accident that the women feed me? God provides. When He is ready He will speak and I must be here to listen."

In the few days that he had been there with the old man the latter had never spoken so much. Aurelius was not sure that he was glad to have heard all this. Some things are best left alone. He would leave if that would not have been interpreted in the village as flight, as a sign of his guilt. Besides, he felt some gratitude, some debt, for the old man having taken him in and fed him. Still, the man was irritating as well as frightening. He was so sure!

"How can you know the ways of the divine one, Alvitus? Even if He did speak once, what makes you positive that He will speak to you again? And if it was a dream you are wasting your life sitting in the dirt and praying to the wind."

The answer this time was long in coming. Waiting for it, the youth could hear the far shrill of the hawk, the hum of the bees, the wind stirring the thatch of the hut. When it did finally come, the holy man spoke in a voice so faint that Oro could not be sure that he heard what he did.

"The time is close now, Aurelius. I have had a sign that He is ready. He sent you to me. That is the sign. Why do you think that I took you into my house?"

# Chapter Ten

That was when I should have left, Aurelius thought. The man is crazy! He doesn't know anything about me. I didn't tell him that I'm an exile. I haven't told him about my uncle. Uncle said that last night in Oveido that people would try to use me, manipulate me, because of my royal blood, but this old nut does not know about that. He couldn't. I think that he couldn't. And what would he have in mind if he did? How could I be a sign of anything? A sign of trouble—that's all I have been since I left Oviedo.

But I haven't been able to leave here. It is a little like being caught in a dream again. I don't really believe that Alvitus is crazy. He scares me mostly just because he isn't. But for some reason I can't even run away. Why is it that I have this strange feeling that something important is about to happen to me here? I ought to go into his sacred woods, poke around in there and stir up his spirit, his ghost or whatever it is! But I don't. Ever since I stopped being a baby I've been at home in the forest. When I've been lonely, like now, it has been my favorite place. Yet all of a sudden I'm frightened to enter one—this one anyway.

Nor, he had noticed, was he alone in this feeling. The villagers gave that place a wide berth as well. The women did their wash well downstream of where the old man sat and stared. They did not even walk up into the forest verge for privacy when they needed to wash their own bodies. They posted a sentry on the bank instead to warn off any too-curious men of the village.

Nor did Oro choose to walk upstream when he bathed himself. He had been embarrassed for it. More than once he had been surprised by the women coming down to wash and had to beat a hasty retreat, gathering up his tunic as he went.

"Don't run off, boy!" Some of the bolder of them had called after him. "Turn about and give us a look. Let a girl have a peek at what you've got."

So he had to travel a good distance indeed to hunt when, ordinarily, he would have simply walked into the forest's edge. He continued to avoid the village because there could be nothing but trouble in such contact until the matter of his identity was settled. But he knew that they watched him as countryfolk watch every stranger. He was never out of their sight for very long and he knew that they noticed that he too avoided old Alvitus' forest. They probably laughed at him for it.

So between skirting the forest on the one hand and the village on the other, Oro felt like a goat on a tether. He was live bait. Someone was going to come along and drag him off—to what he didn't know. And Alvitus had the other end of the rope. The holy man held him there without apparent effort or attention. He is waiting for me to say something. But what?

"The other day you said that I was a sign, Alvitus. You even said that God had sent me. But I have no sense of that. I know how I came to be here but you don't. Actually you can't imagine why I'm here. Can you tell me for what purpose you imagine that I have been sent?"

The morning had hardly begun. But ever since the cocks

of the village had begun their pre-dawn racket, Aurelius had been awake and pondering how to approach the old man. He sensed that he was expected to do that but he really didn't want to. Yet the longer he did not the more the tension between them built. He could not leave and he could not remain silent any longer. They sat together, facing the wood, and sharing some cold porridge from a pot.

"I don't imagine, Oro. Country bumpkins imagine. Imagination is useless in such matters. I simply know that you were sent to me. I can't tell you how I know that. But it is true. And I think that you are beginning to realize that it is true. I can hear that much in your voice."

"But why am I here?"

"To help me. I would guess that. You are to be my assistant. You are to be my disciple in my calling."

"But you don't even know what your own calling is! What am I supposed to help you with?

"We will be told that when it is time, Oro. Must I tell you that over and over? We are called first to patience, you and I. That is the first lesson. That is the first road. To be silent and to listen. That is the whole of our task for the present. God will fill the silence when He chooses. Until then, we can do nothing."

The young man was horrified. The spell that surrounded him—had for days, perhaps since his arrival—was almost paralyzing him. He had to throw it off.

"What if I told you that I'm a rapist? That that is the reason that I'm here. What if I had to flee from my home because they wanted to execute me for raping a young girl?"

"Are you a rapist, Aurelius? Or do you make this up, to annoy me or to disgust me? You can tell me if it makes you feel better but it does not matter. If God has chosen you it does not matter what you have done before now. Paul the

Apostle began as a murderer, did he not? It is no business of mine to say yes or no. Or better, it is my business only to say yes. No matter where that leads us, you and I."

"No, I'm not a rapist but I was almost tried for one back in Oviedo. They would have killed me if I hadn't run for it."

No matter what he said the net kept closing. Aurelius felt as the pheasant must when the unsuspected strands suddenly leap from the ground and block off the way to the sun. What if it were some evil trap? What if Alvitus were a wizard or a very devil instead of a real holy man?

"Then what if I tell you that I am the nephew of Alfonso, king in Oviedo? It is the king who has sent me to Galicia, to Count Muño, to keep me safe from enemies of the crown? What then becomes of your precious knowledge? Your revelation did not tell you that! Do you think to meddle with the purposes of the king himself. You play a dangerous game, old man."

"Have you royal blood, indeed, Oro? What a stange thing that would be. But your royal uncle has no part in this, I think. He is no matter to me or to you. King Alfonso sent you? God sent you still. It is the same thing. Have you never heard the saying, 'God writes straight with crooked lines'? Be quiet, young man. If you aren't quiet you are going to miss something that you should hear. Just shut up and listen, my young friend! Just shut up and be still! Hold your tongue and your breath, stop your heart, and look inside. See the chasm! See the abyss, the abyss of your soul, and be very still!"

"No! Wait, Alvitus! You don't know! You don't know!"

Oro knew that he had to stop this. The old man was leading him where he did not wish to go. He felt dizzy, as if there were actually the precipice that the other spoke of and he was on its brink.

"I killed a deer. On the way to here I killed a buck. It jumped out in front of me and I killed it before I even thought. It was what I always wanted to do, ever since I was old enough to hunt. But afterwards, I couldn't use it. It was too heavy to carry. Its meat was too tough to eat, most of it anyway. The pelt began to stink because I didn't know how to cure it. I finished by throwing it away. All my life I wanted to kill a buck and when I did, I didn't know what to do with it. It was just stupid! I was just stupid."

He was close to tears. Why was he close to tears? Alvitus wasn't going to answer him. He had said this dumb thing and the old man was going to let it hang there between them. God, he was humiliated! It wasn't right that the old man shouldn't even answer him. He could say something. He could put some distance between them and those stupid words he'd blurted out. But the silence did end—finally.

"All your life? How old are you, Oro, fifteen? You did something stupid and it humiliated you. That happens to every young man sooner or later. At least there was no one there to see it. You don't have to tell anyone about it, you know. Don't make yourself so important. It's over and done and no one really cares."

The youth could have struck him. The arrogant old bastard! Nothing mattered to him except his silly belief that he was special, chosen. Actually he was stupid. Oro had told him the story so that the old man would see that he was just an ordinary person, that there was nothing special about him. But the holy man had missed the point! Alvitus was so sure about everything and he had not understood at all.

For a long time they sat silently in the waxing sun. It warmed their shoulders, then their backs.

"There was this woman. She saved my life. Her husband picked me up sick from the side of the trail and she fed me, warmed me, coaxed me back to life. But I stabbed her, cut her! I didn't mean to but she kept pressing up to me. She wanted love from me. Her husband was out. She was old and fat and ugly. I hated her! So I cut her with my knife and then I ran. That's how I got here!"

Had the skinny little hermit sighed? Was that what he had just heard? No, probably not. That would have been too human. Alvitus was a rock. He was a hard knot of dried muscle and aging bone. There was no moisture in him—no give. He did not have enough softness in his entire body to allow him a sigh. But did he finally understand?

"You seem to think, young man, that I am a priest. I am not. If you want forgiveness for your sins you will have to find someone else. Do you think that your dirty little secrets, your pathetic catalog of mostly imaginary vices make you unfit for what you have been called to do here? You are a fool, to boot! No one is worthy here. Not I, certainly, not Saint Peter himself if he were sitting sniveling in your place.

"Nothing is important but the plain fact that, for some reason neither one of us understands, God has told us to wait upon Him here. And that is what we shall do. While we do that, try to guard a decent silence. Your complaints only serve to distract me and to distract you yourself from our listening and our waiting. Put everything else away."

His voice trailed off and Oro knew that he would not soon speak again. It was useless. The heat of the day increased. All of its sounds were far off, faint. He was not sure that he could sleep sitting up. Nevertheless, he felt a curiously dream-like state creeping over him. What was it that waited just beyond the edge of that flickering conciousness he could only vaguely focus? He could neither strain towards it nor call it up. But he was aware of a presence nonetheless. It did not menace but he was apprehensive still.

The blow took him unaware. The staff laid across his shoulders had force sufficient to knock him sideways in the dirt. As the shock of it faded, the pain of his shoulders jerked him back to full awareness of his surroundings. There was a small crowd in a semi-circle about Alvitus and himself. Warriors! At least, from the look of their swords and spears they were warriors. They were too well-armed to be bandits. And in the midst of them, a huge man sitting on a horse scarcely equal to his weight. If he were a bit taller, his toes would have dragged in the dust.

Count Muño. It could not be anyone else. Eyes like black stones peered over a huge beak of a nose and were set between a generous head of graying black hair held in long strands and an equally full but free-flowing beard of the same hue. Massive arms and hands toying with the reins were banded with rings of copper studded with precious stones. He held no weapons but a young man stood at his side with sword, shield, bow and quiver, all richly embellished. A cape of splendid silks was thrown back to reveal a worn leather jacket over plain linen tunic and thick leather boots below.

"Get up, boy."

The voice was accustomed to being obeyed but Aurelius could not. There was no feeling in his legs. The numbness of long-sitting had left them useless. They were beyond his control for the moment and he could but scrabble comically in the dust. A couple of the warriors, out of the range of the count's vision, allowed themselves a smile.

"Get him on his feet. Pick the wretch up."

And the nearest of the count's men sprang to do just that. One on each side, they hauled him up by the arms and kept him erect although his legs continued to dangle helplessly beneath him.

"Now tell me who you are, boy, and what business you have in Galicia."

"He says that he is your cousin, lord, and that he has come from Oviedo."

The headman of the village, Miro, volunteered the information. The count turned to fix him with a stare.

"Tip me over that insolent peasant."

The nearest warrior sprang into action. With one hand he pressed his short sword to the startled man's belly while with the other he clasped his crutch. For a moment there followed a semi-comic shoving match which ended abruptly when the increasing pressure of the blade signaled to Miro that the man was perfectly willing to stab him through. The village chief released his hold on his crutch and the warrior struck him solidly with the flat of the sword. The other tottered and then losing his balance fell heavily. The warrior bestrode him.

"If he ventures another word, cut the old bastard's throat."

Count Muño turned his attention to Aurelius once again. Enough time had passed meanwhile for the young man to have recovered the use of his legs and the warriors hesitated, unsure whether or not to release him.

"Stand back from the chicken. He's not about to harm us and it's too soon to pluck him." The count's tone was even, contemptuous. "Once again, boy, tell me who you are and what you are doing here. Speak up."

"I am Aurelius, greatnephew of King Aurelius, and cousin of King Alfonso who now rules in Asturias, Galicia, Cantabria, and Oviedo. On the orders of my uncle—cousin—the king, I have come to claim the hospitality of the great Count Muño, lord of Galicia under the king."

"My, my, my! Such a great one for an almost naked

stripling whom I find daydreaming in the dust next to an old faker. Do you know that it is treason to claim royal descent, boy? Do you know what the penalty is for treason? I can have you chopped up for dog-meat—a little at a time. Maybe I will unless you can prove to me real quickly that you are who you say. Why should I believe all this raving done by a frightened lad scarcely out of a child's years?"

"I have knowledge of the court of the king at Oviedo because I lived there before coming here. I can tell you who his main advisers are among the nobles. I can tell you which of the bishops that he has named still retain his trust. I can even describe for you how he is accustomed to dress when he holds a crown-wearing at Christmas, or Easter, or Pentecost. I can tell you what his favorite foods are, if you wish it."

The bulky potentate's eyes narrowed yet more at Oro's words. For a moment he had no reply. When he did, the count chose his words very carefully.

"Can you tell me so much, boy? Then you have knowledge, interested knowlege, of what any noble who plots against or in behalf of the king would need to have. So you know something of the politics of the kingdom. It may be the death of you. As for the rest of that court twaddle, we have more to do than study it, out here beside the western ocean. I would have no way of knowing whether what you told me was true or not."

"The king has two other cousins in his line for succession. Their names are Ramiro and Nepotian. I grew up with them. Ramiro is the son of the old king, Vermudo. Nepotian is the greatnephew of King Fruela who ruled before my own greatuncle. I can tell you what they look like."

Aurelius was becoming desperate. He needed some proof, some fact that would convince this magnate who seemed to become more and more hostile. The count had not dismounted or given any other sign of more than passing interest in his story. He shifted impatiently in his saddle.

"For an old man who never took a wife, King Alfonso is very well supplied with heirs of the blood, don't you think, young man? So he probably wouldn't miss you very much, would he? Every schemer in the kingdom knows that story. I'm beginning to think that you are a spy. Maybe old King Alfonso has sent you here to test my loyalty. Or perhaps some one of my loving rivals has sent you to implicate me in some plot, some treason. Killing you might be the safest thing to do.

"The only reason why I haven't so far is because you seem to be so stupid. What kind of a king's cousin comes without retainers, almost without clothes, into my domains with such a story? Or what kind of a spy, a plotter, enters my territories and does not seek me out but settles down with a crazy old shepherd and makes me come to him? Are you really stupid, boy, or cunning? Or are you simply mad like your master here? Madmen can be dangerous in their own fashion. Or are you simply pretending to be simpleminded to draw me in? It is safer, I think, just to have you killed."

During the course of that long speech it dawned on Aurelius that he was actually being tried. The count now was speaking not so much to him as to the others present. He was explaining his reasons in case he might be making a mistake. Count Muño was getting ready to have him killed right here. He had to find some way to convince him to stop, to wait.

"King Alfonso did send me with proof. He gave me your name and told me to seek you out. He said that you were loyal to him. At Oviedo there was a plot against the king that involved some of his counselors but the king was not sure which ones. He needed time. But the plotters were planning to force my execution because of my royal lineage. The king sent me secretly and alone from the city at night. He gave me a signet ring of his which he said you would recognize. But on my journey here I became ill and the ring was stolen from me by the people who took me in. Or I think they did. So when I came here and you were away hunting, I did not seek out your palace because your servants would not have believed me."

The words poured out of Oro in a torrent. He was arguing for his life and his time was almost spent. He could feel that, but he could see as well that he had given his judge pause, for a moment anyway.

"Plots at court are like crows at harvest, sonny. There's never any shortage of either. Tell me, for what crime were these schemers you mention going to try to force your condemnation."

"Rape, my lord. They claimed I raped a girl but I didn't."

The barest trace of a smile played about the count's lips for a moment.

"Rape? Did they think anybody would believe that you were up to that, boy? Maybe the other way around. Some girl threatened your virtue did she?"

Guffaws greeted the count's sally. Aurelius found himself blushing. Muño noted it and continued.

"Tell me about the king's ring, young man. Tell me all about it."

"It was a signet ring, my lord. Most of it was made of gold with a pearl set on either side of the seal. The seal itself was made of some harder metal, I don't know what, and bore a reproduction of the cross that King Alfonso had made for the bishop's church in the city. The cross was the one consecrated to mark the king's victory over the Africans on the ocean in the south about Lisbon."

The count had listened closely to the young man, now sweating profusely as he argued for his life.

"I know the ring, boy. Why shouldn't I. The king and I shared that campaign. After our victory I helped him loot the very pearls that grace the cross on which he modeled it. Tell me again what happened to it."

"The ring disappeared while I was sick. I had a fever. When I woke it was gone. A charcoalburner and his wife took care of me. It was in the mountains to the south of Lugo. When I recovered a little, I fled from there."

Oro told just so much of his story as he could without completely humiliating himself. He wasn't really accusing anyone. But he couldn't admit that he had fled from the old lady and had not even thought about the ring until later. He couldn't tell them that he had been afraid to go back. But the tale appeared to satisfy the count partially. After he had thought for a bit, that noble arrived at a course of action.

"Just as well you ran, boy. They would have probably cut your throat at some point. Especially if you asked them about the ring. Likely it's the richest piece of work they ever saw in their miserable lives.

"That is, if there is any truth at all in what you have told me. I'm of two minds about you, young man. For one, you may simply be what you say you are. That doesn't seem likely but it is just possible. On the other hand, you are very deeply into something. I do believe that you have come from Oviedo and that you know the life of the court there. So, if you are a spy or an intriguer, you are a very dangerous one.

"Either way you are going to put me to a little trouble. I am going to send off some of my more trustworthy companions to Oviedo to make inquiries about you to the king himself. If you are what you say, well and good. If you are something or someone else, you are going to bitterly regret it for the brief time that you will live. Until their return, you will not leave this village. Every other day you will come to my palace so that I may be satisfied that you have not run off.

And don't run off. You won't get enough start and my trackers will find you no matter how hard you try to escape. Believe me. When they do, I'll have you taken apart joint by joint. Whatever it is that you are trying to do, there is no way out for you now. Either you will be a king's cousin or you will be carrion. Count on me for that."

Having said so much, the count neck-reined his pony and kicked it into motion. "You, old man," he said to Alvitus, "See that your young companion does not disappear. I hold you responsible."

"If you want a guard, leave one of those thugs you take such pride in," came the answer. "I am not reponsible to you or anyone else. I have no time for your bloody nonsense."

The silence that fell was immediate and profound. Count Muño stiffened and, for a moment, it appeared that he was about to turn his horse into the hermit. Then he thought better of it and began to ride off, shaking his shaggy head.

"Let that old fool up," he called to the warrior who still stood over Miro. The village chief glared in the direction of Aurelius as he did not dare to do after the retreating count. In that look the young man saw that he could be sure of the close surveillance of that one at least. He was unused to having someone hate him personally and it made him even more uncomfortable than the cold menace of the count.

A few minutes later, when they were all out of earshot, an Oro shaking with released nervous tension addressed himself shortly and violently to Alvitus.

"You never said a word to help me. Count Muño was ready to kill me and you said nothing at all. You would have sat there like the decaying old stump that you are and never even have raised your voice in my behalf."

"Despite what your fears tell you, you were never in any danger, young man," came the response. "Do you think that God would permit that great ignorant barbarian to interfere with what He is about here? Sit down now. Take a deep breath. Take several deep breaths and hold the last of them until you can hold it no longer. Let the eye of your mind watch the terrors of your body disappear. In any event, you defended yourself quite agilely."

There was just the least hint of amusement in the dry tones of the old man's final words. Aurelius could not believe it. Could he have imagined it?

"So now you see, my young friend how even the bloody suspicions of that man of craft and violence work to confirm your calling. Not long ago you were considering running off because of your fear of me. Your fear of God really. And now that evil beast has sentenced you to remain here for how long? How long will it take his messengers to travel to Oviedo and back? Four weeks? Five weeks? Six?

"They won't strain themselves. Plenty of time for the Lord to work His will here, whatever that may be. You and I must redouble our watching to be ready for it."

I am like a bird charmed by a snake, Aurelius thought. The old man holds me with his eyes and with his confidence. I would rather be anywhere than here. But even while he pondered the last thought the young man had to fight back the realization that there was, deep inside him, the stirring of an attraction to the mysterious course of events that the hermit foresaw.

# Chapter Eleven

For three hours now he had been walking and the sun was almost directly overhead. Each step took him into his own shadow and soon enough it would be behind him. A line of perspiration marked the shoulders of his tunic but he was comfortable as he swung along. It felt good to get the stiffness out of his legs. Not that the long discipline of watching with Alvitus hadn't become more bearable. Those extended periods of concentration had given him another, new sort of exercise. He was more conscious of the little things coming about in the world of nature about him. At the same time, that heightened awareness of nature around him had less and less power to distract, as if it were taking place in the underwater world of a pool and he was swimming in it but, at the same time, it was not his own element. There was a sort of perfect clarity about what transpired but it all happened in a crystal sphere remote from his person even while it was utterly transparent.

Yet each time when he slowly unfolded himself from that quiet state his young muscles screamed for motion and lubrication. Two days had passed since his first encounter with Count Muño and he was secretly happy to have an excuse to escape the regimen that Alvitus was pressing upon him. He was sure that Alvitus knew how he felt but the old man could not object with any hope of success so he had kept his silence and his dissatisfaction to himself. So, for a day, he was free.

The distance to the count's palace had been considerable. But the world about him was green and warm and boiling with the life of early summer and he had nothing to do except to enjoy its sights, its sounds, and its smells. He hadn't even gotten hungry. Well, not much anyway. The spare diet he shared with Alvitus, the leavings of the women of the village, occasionally made him long for the food of the hunt. Aurelius was sure that the food at the palace would be richer than that, and a great deal more ample he hoped.

He knew that he was hard upon his destination. Clearings in the fields were becoming more frequent and rather larger. Smoke was more noticeable in the heavy air. Then he came in sight of a sizable collection of beehive-shaped huts. The people here about apparently felt no fear for there was no sign of earthwork or timber defenses. Dogs out now showed no particular interest in him. At night it might have been different. Well beyond the village itself he could see a much larger structure set on a hillside. Its timbered walls resting on a solid stone foundation rose to more than three times a man's height and must be four times as long as it was tall, he thought. The roof thatch was gray with age where it could be seen through the moss and grass that grew heavy upon it. A little to the right sat a strong tower all of stone and roofed with slates that rose another man's height above the ridgeline of the roof of the palace itself.

Before he reached it he found himself passing a blacksmith's forge and the squat practitioner of that art was banging lustily on what might be a piece of iron destined to become a dagger. There were a few more small huts just beyond here and well before reaching the palace itself. Somewhat down the hill he could see as well as smell the latrine pits which were set well away from the great hall. This was an old settlement and a permanent one from the looks of it. Behind all there was an enclosed corral where four or five shaggy ponies had trampled the muddy grass into a near swamp. A barn opened onto the corral and now that he was closer, he could see the dome-shaped earthen oven set forty or so paces away from the timbered hall and its thatch. All the surroundings bespoke a great noble very much at home here.

"You there! Yes, you! Hold up right there!"

A well-muscled man of middle age had gotten up from lounging in front of one of the huts. He advanced on Oro idly swinging the cudgel that marked him as a bailiff. The man squinted as he came, trying better to focus the eyes that bore the tell-tale pale webby film of the spider's illness.

"What are you doing hanging around the palace of the count? Strangers and other thieves are not welcome here. You had best make yourself scarce before I call some of the young studs hereabout to run you off."

"I have been commanded by the count to attend upon him every third day. He wishes that way to know that I have not tried to flee the district."

"You mean that our count takes an interest in young men hardly come of age and clad in dirty and ragged tunics? More likely that I'm the king of the Africans at Córdoba."

"No, sir. Really, I'm supposed to report to your count after each second day. He told me that himself. He'd be angry if I didn't and angry, perhaps, with you if you did not let me see him."

The heavy man had gotten in front of him now and seemed inclined to prevent him physically from going on farther. Oro was not sure about the wisdom of pushing past him but it was beginning to look as if that might be necessary.

"Well then, you can give me your name, sonny, and I'll tell him that you were here. You just do that and then go back to wherever you came from. Do you have a name? And does the count know it?"

Why, wondered Jimena, is my father's bailiff harassing that pretty young man? The old fellow was so tiresome. More so every day. It would be fun to upset him for a change.

"Britto, does that young gentleman have business with my father?"

"He claims that he does, my lady, but he has no proof of that. From the look of him I'd say that he is no gentleman. For sure not." Taken unaware, the bailiff instinctively put himself on the defensive.

"You may be right, Britto. After all, how many gentlemen do we ever see here? You might not be able to tell one if you saw him. For that matter, none of us might be able to recognize one."

She smiled sweetly at the bailiff who nonetheless understood that he was being rebuked. Still, the man stood his ground. Ignoring him, Jimena turned now to Oro.

"Are you a gentleman, indeed, sir? Do we treat you hardly? Will you think ill of us?" In all of this her tone alternated ever so lightly between the mock serious and the mocking.

Aurelius was speechless. This girl had come from nowhere and now wanted an answer of him. He did not even know that he was staring. Britto did though, and frowned mightily. This was a princess surely. Well, a countess perhaps. If he could have told where her rich, auburn hair curling in such profusion down across her shoulders ended and her scalp began, she might be a few fingers shorter than he. But he could hardly measure her too close since the deep green of her eyes danced about his face and seemed to scan him all at once from head to toes.

She was clad in a simple, linen, he thought, tunic of a green that matched her eyes but was edged, it seemed to him, in a fine stitching of gold thread. The cloth lay easily against her breasts but it was sleeveless for the season and short, perhaps for convenience in riding. Would she ride? Did great ladies do that here in Galicia beside the ocean? In any event, her arms and legs showed the naturally pale skin of the fair-haired but were colored with the onset of summer to a rich, dark cream. Like goat's milk.

"Come, sir!" Her voice was mock peremptory. "You are not polite to ignore one who has taken an interest in your sorry state here. I could almost believe that the bailiff was right."

"I'm not sure, Mam, that anyone ever asked if I were a gentleman before." He managed to stammer so much out and then cursed himself silently for such a stupid reply.

"Well then, perhaps it is time that someone did. But you must give me an answer before my father's steward here decides to drive you from our land."

Jimena knew that she was teasing outrageously. Britto was furious and this very pleasant-looking young man was so confused that he could hardly speak. But it was good fun and she loved to flirt—as she was discovering now that she had a possibly interesting candidate.

"Well, my lady, I am a cousin to King Alfonso in Oviedo. But I think that the count—your father?—does not believe that. He has sent men to inquire of my uncle about me and meanwhile has forbidden me to leave the district. He has also ordered that I come here every third day so that he may be sure that I have not run off to make mischief elsewhere."

The words seemed impossibly stupid to Oro. He would

not believe them if he were the girl. But she surprised him again. She bowed her head, just a fraction, as if to acknowledge his claim of royal blood. Then, almost like a denial of what she had just done, she shook her head, setting that mass of auburn hair aswirl.

"Oh, you're that one. The king's nephew that has gotten religion and lives with the old hermit in the village beyond the hills." This in seemingly high seriousness. And then, with a slight smile, "Has no one cared to cover the king's nephew in a new tunic? That one is filthy, don't you know? No wonder my father doesn't believe you. I hardly can myself. Come along after me. We'll get you one that may impress my father. He can hardly see you looking like that."

And with that, Jimena bounded off—well, she definitely started at a bound. But she thought better of it.... Be more controlled. I don't think that I can manage stately in this summer tunic. But I had best not act like a little girl either.

At one of the smaller huts she found Muña, a laundress, where she always was at noon. Sneaking a small nap. Jimena gave directions quickly to the confused woman. "We need a tunic for this gentleman, Muña. Something that befits his station. He has a meeting arranged with my father for this noon and we can't let him go in looking like this can we?"

"No, my lady." She could not imagine this ragged young man—not ugly though—as having an interview with the count. Still less did he resemble a gentleman, at least one she'd ever seen. But there were clean tunics, thank God, and she found one shortly. The laundress would have handed it to the fellow but the lady took it from her and passed it with a mischievous smile to Oro.

"Put this one on," she said. And she stood there looking at him as though she expected him to doff his old one and slip on this one right in front of her. He was filled with confusion, as she knew very well that he would be. While he hesitated and she looked at him as if in question, the old laundress took pity on him. The lady was behaving most outrageously. She had these spells. Muña motioned with her head to the hut she had just vacated. "In there, young man."

Ungraciously, Aurelius vanished into it at the instant. When he emerged from the hut a moment later the girl was gone. In her place stood the bailiff, Britto, who motioned him to follow with a jerk of his head. Muña resumed her nap, not without some foreboding. That girl!

The great hall smelled of smoke and dogs. Some little light filtered through the smoke-hole in the thatch high above but it hardly affected the permanent gloom of the spacious interior. No dogs were in sight just then but a couple of warrior-guards lounged about one far end, out of earshot but within easy call. The count sat on a stool close to the wall opposite the doorway and Aurelius followed the bailiff across the straw-covered dirt floor, blinking to adjust his eyes to the shadow.

"This boy, my lord...." Britto began but the count waved him off curtly.

"So you found you way here. Found yourself some new clothes too. It's a good thing that you did come. Shows some sense anyway. Tell the cook to give you something to eat and come back in another two days if you value your health."

The young man tried not to bridle at the abrupt dismissal after his journey of the entire morning. There was no help for it. He would have turned to go but the older man sitting on yet another stool by the count's side addressed him.

"You are the young man who told my brother here that you are a cousin of King Alfonso of Oviedo?"

The man who spoke to him was tall, taller than the count. Once he must have been just as muscular for the bones of his frame were ample. But now his flesh was beginning to sag, as it does with the ones who are starting to age. His tunic was finer, softer than that of the count and his sandals more richly worked than his brother's rough boots. His eyes were equally direct and probing though, and on the right side of his face an old puckered scar ran from the hairline down almost to the bottom of his jaw. Someone long ago had come very close to killing him.

"This is my brother, Teodemiro. He is bishop of Iria Flavia down on the coast. He knows your uncle—if King Alfonso is your uncle."

Count Muño had shown surprise and a little annoyance when his brother had addressed his visitor but now, apparently, had thought better of it. Aurelius, in turn, understood that they had been discussing him. He was, then, more important to them than his perfunctory reception indicated.

"Yes, lord bishop. I am the cousin of King Alfonso and the greatnephew of King Aurelius. You might remember him although I don't."

"Yes, I met him once when I was about the age that you are now. I don't know that I see any resemblance to him in you. But tell me about your cousin, the king. I am told that you sometimes call him uncle. Is he well? Is he still a great patron of churches, a great builder of churches?"

"He is very well, lord bishop. We, my cousins Ramiro and Nepotian and I, are accustomed to call him uncle. The king prefers it himself. He has had three churches built in Oviedo alone, sir. Would you like me to name the three of them and describe what they are like?"

Bishop Teodemiro almost let himself smile. The young man was intelligent. He knew an interrogation when he heard one. Still, lots of villains were intelligent, too intelligent for their own good. Whoever he was, the young man was confident. He probably could describe the king's new churches if I pressed him, mused the bishop. I think I am inclined to believe him but it is better to let my brother's agents decide that.

"No need for that, young man. They have been described to me before in detail. But I've never met your hermit friend. Alvitus they call him. I am told that you have begun to sit with him for long hours. It seems a strange way for a young man to behave. Especially for a healthy one who makes claim to royal blood. Tell me about him."

Oro was not sure that he understood this change of tack. Nor was he sure that he himself knew why he had remained with the old man. How to phrase an answer?

"When I first arrived in Galicia, sir, I had been ill and was still weak. Alvitus was kind to receive me and to share his food with me. The village people about told me that he was once a shepherd. They, some of them—the women-think that he is a holy man. They give him food. He gives some of it to me."

"I know all that, Aurelius, is it? And you know that I know all of that. Don't be evasive with me. What does he tell you? What is he doing there?"

"Lord bishop, he does not talk much. And I don't think that he himself knows what he is doing exactly. What he has told me is that he is waiting for a message from God. I'm sorry. I know it sounds strange but that's what he believes and that what he's doing."

A frown slid over Bishop Teodemiro's face. He moved uneasily on his stool and hesitated before he proceeded. For a moment he seemed reluctant to ask further.

"Has he told you what brings him to be sitting in the dirt on the edge of a forest, sitting and talking with himself?"

"He says that that is what God told him to do. That is why he stopped being a shepherd and became a holy man."

"So you think that he is a holy man too? What exactly did this God of his tell him? When was that? When will this new message come?"

"I'm sorry, sir. He doesn't know when something will happen—just that he has to wait. And he didn't say when exactly he got his message. All he has said to me is that he doesn't know how he knows. It just came to him."

"You are no fool, young man. You know how strange all of this sounds to me and my brother. This Alvitus could be a lunatic. He could be dangerous. He could be dangerous to himself and to everyone connected with him. You could pay a very steep price for that little bit of hospitality he showed you once. Why are you staying there? Why do you join your person to that of a madman?"

The bishop had leaned forward, visibly agitated. His brother, the count was also intent. There was no room for an easy answer here.

"I do not think that he is mad, sir. He is very calm, very quiet. He just sits quietly and waits. He isn't doing anything that would disturb, that would harm, anyone. He prays. He prays out loud sometimes, in Latin. I sit with him sometimes because there is a kind of peace in it. There is a stillness that comes over you from inside of yourself. And I have to wait anyway. By order of your brother."

Oro finished lamely. He knew that but it seemed to him that it would be very dangerous now to mention that Alvitus believed that he himself had been sent to help with whatever was to happen. It would certainly be insane to say that sometimes he had begun to believe it himself.

His words hung in the air. Bishop Teodemiro stared hard

at him, then decided against speaking. He looked at his brother who returned his glance and nodded.

"Tell the cook to give you something to eat. Then you can leave but come back again as I've said."

Oro bowed slightly. It didn't seem like a bad idea to be as polite as he could. He reflected as he left the hall that Alvitus might be in greater trouble than he was himself. They were beginning, he thought, to believe him but they were never going to believe the old man.

The fat cook in the blackened kitchen beyond the hall gave him a cold joint of roast goat and a large piece of bread. It was oven baked bread, not the rock-bread they sometimes got from the villagers. His mouth began to water as soon as he saw it. Despite his now raging appetite, he forced himself to eat slowly. As he did so, sitting on the ground alongside the wall of the great hall, he looked about busily for the girl. But she never came into sight. He wondered if she were watching him. After a bit that idea made him increasingly nervous and finally he could delay no longer. The meat and the bread were gone. His excuse for tarrying vanished, he rose and left.

# Chapter Twelve

"So they sent me back my monk."

I must, Alvitus thought, talk more to the boy. There is a willingness in him now that was not there at first but it is still hard for him. If I forget how young he is I may spoil him—the thing he is meant to be. Since he was sent to me, doesn't that mean that I am intended to mold him, to form him? I know that there is a danger of arrogance in thinking that. I suppose too that arrogance has always been my besetting vice. Still, he wants gentling—like a new lamb. He is not yet ready to live in full silence. He doesn't hear his own voices. He doesn't hear your voice, my Lord. Or he will not hear it if ever You decide to speak.

"They did not send me back," Aurelius was saying. "I came back because my errand was done. I came back because I prefer it here."

"But you went away eagerly enough, I thought. You find your vocation here a burden sometimes."

He could just be silent, Aurelius thought. God knows he is silent often enough. He goes for days without a word and then he suddenly chooses to bait me.

"I found that they do not much care for you there. The count has a brother, the bishop in Iria Flavia, who is much interested in you but I do not think in your good health."

"So you have met Bishop Teodemiro? That one is a man of blood—like his brother. No, he is not likely to approve of me. He couldn't begin to understand what I am doing."

"You say that he is a man of blood?"

"Yes. He was born to it. Like the count. They both grew up with swords in their hands. They were both first trained by their father as warriors. The old count was outraged that his oldest son should choose the church instead of the battlefield. Not that one is so different than the other the way they rule it.

And the bishop has not entirely forgotten what they drilled into him as a boy. You've seen the scar on his face? Well, the man who gave it to him is dead. He was a young monk, too young I think. Anyway he was keeping a woman on the side. The bishop learned of it and commanded him to put her away. The monk said that he would obey. All very proper. Then one night he attacked the bishop at his own dinner table with a knife. Opened up the side of his eminence's face with a single blow. But it was the last offense he ever committed. The bishop blocked his arm and then gutted the monk with a serving knife. Those reflexes from the training ground never leave you."

"But he was just defending himself. You are not being fair to him."

"Fair to him? Let God be fair to the old tyrant, if He wants to be. Did Christ defend himself? Did you ever hear from the pulpit that one of the apostles gutted a Roman executioner while defending himself? The bishop is a man of blood. That's the long and short of it. He sees himself as a judge and maybe as a general. He has lost sight of what it is to sit in the presence of the Lord and tremble for one's lost innocence. He cannot be expected to understand or approve of what we are about, you and I."

So there is a passion in you yet, thought Oro. Maybe it would be a good thing if I found out how much.

"And what if they came for you, Alvitus? You do sound just a little as though you too have known something of the warrior's field. If they were going to kill you—if they were going to interfere with the work that you think God is trying to do here -wouldn't you perhaps be tempted to a little violence to protect it? To let it go forward?"

The holy man actually half-turned toward him. He leaned forward just a bit and looked at Aurelius. Never had the young man seen him come so far out of his habitual reserve.

"Why do you think that I sit here, Oro? Is it because I like to have my muscles cramp up and my stomach scream for real food, not those scraps and parings that the old ladies leave for us? Yes, I would be tempted. The natural man is alive in me too. That's why I train. That's why you must train. So that the fleshly man in us can be restrained from presuming to help God. The bishop thinks that he can do the work of God! That's his problem and a sacrilege. That is why I call him a man of blood.

"Listen to me. A long time ago I was a soldier. I was even a good soldier and I did the things a soldier does. I killed people. They were the enemy. They were bad people, or so we thought. So we were taught. So I made them bleed for it. You and your poor little deer! These were men, some of them women, and I chopped them down. I speared them. I stabbed them. But there were always more of them. We never lacked for enemies. No one ever lacks for enemies! Finally, it made me sick.

"So I left it. I left the whole world. I despised what men and women do to one another. The cruelties! The hatreds! I went out alone with my sheep to the hills and the high pastures. I listened to the wind and watched the clouds and kept my own counsel. I pondered the scripture lessons that I had heard and I sang the Psalms to my sheep. Maybe I went a little crazy.

"That life taught me to want little and to live with less. I would be there still if God had not seized hold of me one day and shaken me until my whole mind and body ached. I thought that He would kill me but He was only teaching me that I was not free. When He turned me loose I knew that I was to come here and wait for His return. What is to come here soon will be stopped by no count and by no bishop.It may destroy them. It may destroy you and I. But it will be an act of God. Not of any man."

Ooh! thought Alvitus. This young man takes me out of myself. He tempts me to break through the self control I've been working at this whole while to convince him by main force. There's too much passion, too much will, in me yet. Help me to sit still, Lord! Help me to be quiet before your face!

As the hermit gradually drew away, drew himself into himself, Oro felt the excitement dying in himself as well. I shouldn't bait the old man. I shouldn't try to bring him back from where he is going. Even if I can't follow him there yet. When I just sit and keep him company, or keep his body company, I have this feeling of peace. There isn't anything very much that I need. The village and the villagers are very far away. A little more quiet, a bit more emptying out of myself and I could be within the forest, its green and its shade, its solitude and its mystery.

* * *

The two days just past had been the most serene of his young life. He could hardly recall their passing. They had become one continuing present. Aurelius had woken from them as if from a sleep of dream. He wanted to will himself back into them by the sheer force of his mind but he could not. Finally, he knew that he must journey once again to the palace of Count Muño and register his obedience. The prospect at first filled him with misgiving. They would ask him again about Alvitus and he was not sure how best he could answer them. If the old man was supremely confident of his own safety, Oro was not so sure. What might happen if the count, or the bishop, decided to have the hermit murdered? Or if they signaled secretly to the villagers that Alvitus would have no protection from them? If he said the wrong thing or gave the wrong impression, he might become an accomplice in the old man's murder!

Should he pretend himself to believe that Alvitus was just a harmless old eccentric? Could he bring himself to lie convincingly that way about his own feelings? Should he admit to them that he believed rather that the hermit was truly a man of God and hope that they would be afraid therefore to act against his teacher? Or would the fear that it was really a holy man that they had on their hands drive them to some immediate action? He could come to no conclusion. Every path seemed wrong. Every solution held its own dangers.

As he walked, pondering, his gait began to increase almost without his willing it consciously. The colors of the trail became more vivid and the song of the birds richer and more detailed. And then he remembered. The girl. Would he get to see her once again? He had no need to try to remember her appearance. It was as present to him, suddenly, as if no time at all had passed since their last encounter. In his mind's eye, those auburn tresses stirred again and the green eyes sparkled with secret emotion. She might just have been laughing at him.

When the palace of the count first came into view his eyes sought first for her. To no avail. Instead he encountered the bailiff, Britto, whose demeanor had not improved greatly over their first encounter. Nevetheless the man showed him into the presence of the count in the great hall. Oro had thought that the bishop might be there but Count Muño was alone save for two warriors whom he waved off at the young man's approach. To the latter's surprise, the features of the noble softened ever so slightly.

"Well, Aurelius, your wardrobe has improved. Perhaps that is a sign that your conduct will also."

"The tunic is proof of the generosity of your house, my lord. I can take no credit for it but I am grateful."

Oro had no idea whether or not the count knew of the gesture of his daughter or even if he might have directed her to act so. He hoped not. But it was best to assume that little went on in the palace or its surroundings of which the great man was unaware.

"Gratitude is a scarce virtue in my experience, Aurelius. And equally rare is the man who understands the full obligations of his station in life. Men in whom you put your trust get all blown up with their own importance and then are all the more likely to behave without thinking and so bring discredit on their patron as well as themselves."

Polite chatter was not what Oro had come to expect from this rude, blunt man. He had no sense of what was intended though he knew well enough that this was not mere pleasantry. He responded as ambiguously as he could manage.

"You have more knowledge of men and affairs than I have, my lord."

"But you yourself should have some idea of what is meet. You were raised, or at least you say that you were, in a king's court. One thinks that the cousin of a great king would be careful of his behavior. He would not act so as to bring ridicule upon his cousin's house, do you think?"

"I have tried, sir, to act as my uncle would have me."

The count frowned. He was not comfortable bandying words with a mere lad. He would have to take a direct approach.

"I do not take you for a dull person, Aurelius. Would your uncle, or cousin—call him what you will—have you lodging with a lunatic? A self-styled holy man? Suppose for a moment that people really do take you now for what you say that you are, a person of the royal house. Then the simple ones, at least, will begin to presume that this old faker has the recognition of the king himself. You see the impression you are bound to create? Is that what you intend? Is that what the king would wish? If you claim royal blood then you must be more careful of your actions."

Now he understood. The count was more and more convinced of the truth of his identity, even though word had not yet come from Oviedo. And the more that was so, the more of a problem for the count, and his brother the bishop, his own friendship for Alvitus became. The more likely his royal blood became, the more not only his own safety but that of his teacher's became. Oro was relieved and pleased. He could protect his friend merely by continuing to be his companion. So long as he guarded his own actions he didn't have to worry about arguing in Alvitus' behalf. The thing took care of itself. Very neat! He struggled to keep this new awareness out of his voice as he replied.

"I can see the possible problem, sir, and I will try to take care not to give false impressions. Still, a moment ago you spoke of the duty of gratitude. It would play my uncle's blood false if I were to be less than grateful to the first man I met in Galicia who treated me with kindness."

I was right, Muño thought. This young man is not stupid. He has gained some idea of his own bargaining position. Damn! But there is more than one way to deal with young blood. Even royal blood.

"You are right, young man. Kindness should be rewarded with kindness. But be careful about where it can lead. That old man is no one's fool and he knows how much good a friend at court could do for him. Just don't let him take advantage of your goodness of heart. Remember your responsibility to the king, first and last. Gratitude is a virtue for sure but it comes after duty. Never forget that.

"Now you should eat. Let them know in the kitchen what you would like. I have other matters that need attention. Oh! Do you ride? Surely a young man raised in the palace of a king has learned to ride?"

"Yes sir, I can ride. My uncle saw that my cousins and I were taught."

"Well, if you care to ride after you eat and before you leave, there are some horses in the corral. Poor jades, it may be, for one accustomed to finer horseflesh, but you are welcome to use one of them if you wish it."

"I thank you very much, your lordship. I would like that."

Excused, Oro found his way to the kitchen and dined on garlic-rubbed pork and more oven bread. Even some of the new vintage of the white wine of the country was quietly provided without his asking. The deference that was creeping into these people's relations with him gave him proof again that his person was being accepted for what he said it was. At the very least, people were taking care not to have given offense if it should turn out to be so.

Later, he did make his way to the corral. Whether or not

his ability to ride was another test, he had best act as though he found riding natural. The animals were hardly horses. They were the ponies native to the country. One choice seemed as good as another.

"Do you care for my father's animals?"

How easily he startles, thought Jimena. He has hardly any self-consciousness at all. He is almost impossibly innocent. If he were not so innocent the way he gapes at me would be rude. It is lucky that I chose this gold tunic. It looks good on me and the ribbons of gold silk I used to tie back my hair match it nicely. There are times when I positively love being stared at.

"Father said that you were going riding. I had thought of going myself. Would you mind very much if we rode together? I could show you the good trails and something of our own Galicia. Our hills will be small for you after the mountains of Asturias but you can still get lost in them if you don't know your way."

"That would be very nice—very kind- of you, Miss. I would enjoy your company very much."

Idiot! Could I think of any word but "very?" If she laughs at me I'll.... I'll what? Run away and hide like a little kid?

Maybe her father did tell her. Certainly she has already instructed the groom over there who is putting blankets and saddles on two of the ponies. She didn't wait to ask me! But she did ask me very nicely. She wants to ride with me.

"Well, let's go while there is still some sun then. The brown mare is mine."

He really does stare. He needs some manners. If he is going to do that, then he might as well have something more to stare at.

The groom had brought her mare up and she stepped easily up on the mounting block and threw her leg over its back. Jimena was very aware of just how short her tunic was and how fully it showed a length of thigh. How nice it was to have good legs.

The groom had practically to fold Oro's hand about the reins. The boy was gaping at the lady as the lady knew quite well. He was in for a difficult time, that young man was. The count's daughter knew her own worth, that was sure. Amused, the man made off for the barn. Oro, as if awaking, put his own gelding in motion belatedly and cantered after the girl who was easily thirty lengths ahead of him already and riding with controlled grace.

For some miles they rode, he behind her and Jimena setting the direction and the pace. They rode mostly though fir and boulders. It was that kind of country. But the ponies were used to it and sure-footed. Oro thought once that it would be good to have brought his bow but he saw no animals. He had left it in the kitchen. Probably the land was safe enough by day.

At length, Jimena stopped in a small glade and swung down. By the time he drew up she was wiping down her pony with a bit of rough cloth that she had produced from somewhere. He took advantage of her preoccupation to drink in her body and its motions. God, she was beautiful. He could feel his own excitement. Then she turned, smiling, and tossed him the cloth.

"Your horse is sweating a lot. You must weigh more than you look to. Better wipe him down with this before he takes a chill."

While Aurelius turned to that task, Jimena took her seat on a large granite boulder, half-buried in the soil and its top worn smooth by the wind and water of centuries. The sun had heated the rock and now it warmed her. The late afternoon was lovely and she stretched herself in the sun like a red-gold cat. She was enjoying herself immensely.

As he rubbed down his gelding Oro knew very well that she was inspecting him just as he had her. The idea pleased him but he found it difficult to act unaware. The more he tried to act naturally, the more forced his own actions seemed to become. How was one supposed to act? How did men and women talk to one another—and what about?

He needn't have wondered. When he finally turned from the awkward business of trying to rub down the pony while seeming to ignore her presence, Jimena controlled their conversation from the very beginning.

"Tell me about the royal palace of your kinsman in Oviedo."

"Well, its bigger, of course, and made entirely of stone, not timbered at the top like your father's."

"Not the building, for heaven's sake, not the building! The people of the court, the great ladies and what they wear. What do they do to amuse themselves? That kind of thing."

Again, Oro found himself blushing. Of course! Why did he always misunderstand? But I can't think how to answer.

"I'm sorry. I don't remember. That is, I spent most of my time with my cousins, with Ram and Neppy. We never spent much time with the women of the court. We hunted together. I could tell you about that."

"My father and his companions tell hundreds of stories about the hunt and they all bore me silly. Tell me about your cousins instead. Are they as mature as you? Are they as pretty as you? Do you really like them? Which one do you like the most?"

There! she thought. That will give him something to talk about without forever stammering and looking embarrassed. How nice he seems. He has no airs at all about him. He claims to be royal, and I believe it more than half, but he treats me as though I were some great lady high above him. And don't I love it! Flirting with him is such a pleasant game. He makes me feel a little giddy, half-wild even.

And so, for he didn't know how long, Oro found himself telling her about his cousins while she sat and smiled at him encouragingly. He told her of Ram, how skilled he was at the hunt, how brave, and how much their uncle, the king, seemed to value his counsel. And he spoke to Jimena of the cleverness of his cousin, Neppy, and of his endless store of jokes, and of the scrapes into which he got both Ramiro and himself.

His thoughts continued.... It is so damned difficult to keep my mind focused while she sits there, careless of her person. I can't keep staring over her head but she must know where my eyes want to wander. She'll think I'm some foul-minded soldier or peasant. But she doesn't need to keep making it so difficult for me. She does show off! I'm not imagining that!

Anyway, I'm tired of talking about Ram and Neppy. She apparently thinks that they are great—that they're fine and important—and I'm trying to convince her of it. What if I told her that Ram is a great bully and a braggart? What if I just hint a little about Nepotian being such a coward and a sneak?

"So those are my cousins, lady. At least, they are my cousins if you believe me when I say that I am the cousin of King Alfonso. Do you really believe that now? Or are you just teasing me again?"

She was somewhat taken aback. My, he is a little angry. I'll have to be careful but he's told me so much more about himself than I would ever have dared to ask him. I wonder if he really thinks that those cousins of his are so marvelous?

They must take advantage of him terribly if he is so honest with everyone.

"Do I have to believe you, Aurelius? What shall I call you, Oro? You say that your friends do. And you could call me Jimena, as my friends do. Can't we pretend? If you indeed have royal blood, then I must become your servant and you my master. I think that we get on much better as we have been—with me as a count's daughter and you a mysterious stranger."

Her voice was mock-plaintive but she was serious and Oro knew it. He was sorry to have even raised the question. Her father was right, of course. His family was a burden that he could seldom shed. He rushed to repair the damage.

"My lady, Jimena, I could never be your master. I am just a wandering young man who has found a beautiful maiden in a little village in Galicia. She has bewitched me and the spell that she has cast has left me without memory of my own identity. I will never find it again unless she frees me."

He was aware for the first time since he'd met her, she was blushing. Right up to the roots of that marvelous auburn hair. The old men may well be right when they say that women love flattery more than jewelry. Maybe she is more interested in me than I dared hope.

She couldn't help but notice he had a tongue! He can manage pretty things to say! How nice he could be if we could have more time. She half-laughed, half-giggled with a lilt of genuine pleasure and some mischief and slid a bit carelessly down off the boulder.

"Perhaps I will never let you go. You make such a pretty servant. But we had better get back or you will be walking all night to reach your hut and your old man. And now, if you are my servant, you may help me to remount."

The girl gathered up the trailing reins of her mare and

stood waiting by its side. At first Aurelius could not credit what she had said. She could as easily have used the rock to remount! But then he laced his fingers together and offered his upturned palms. Jimena placed her left foot in them and swung lithely up, her right leg neatly clearing the saddle. In the process, her left leg rested for a moment against his upper arm.

Somehow that brief touch ran the length of both their bodies in an instant. With an uncertain smile and a shaken laugh, the young girl turned the mount quickly and kicked it into motion. Oro stood trembling. Then he mounted to follow. Both of them rode in self-conscious silence until they reached the corral by the palace of her father. The groom appeared to take the horses.

"I need to get my bow and quiver. I left them in the cook's shack."

"Don't leave until I come out again. There is something that I have to give you."

Oro found his weapons where he had left them and then stood about in some confusion. He did not know what to expect. Nothing in the day had gone as he had envisioned. Then Jimena reappeared carrying a small packet. She extended it to him.

"It is your own tunic. I had it washed for you. Now you have two of them. A man of your station should have at least so many."

He stammered his thanks once again and the two parted somewhat awkwardly. Once beyond view he took a minute to examine the tunic. Not only had it been washed but several holes had been repaired neatly. Moreover, along its neckline, sleeves and hem a stitching of heavy red and gold thread had been added in decoration. Very carefully now, he refolded it and placed it among the arrows in his quiver.

# Chapter Thirteen

Alvitus was becoming more and more impatient with him. The hermit could sense the growing lack of attention of his pupil in his meditations. When Oro came back each time from the palace of the count he was slow to settle back into the routine of watchfulness and he had scarcely achieved a decent calm when he began to anticipate mentally his approaching return journey.

The lad certainly isn't likely to have become an admirer of that ugly brute nor of his arrogant brother of a bishop either. But something there is exciting him and drawing him from the life of prayer that he needs. Needs more than he realizes. I can't ask. He wouldn't tell me and that would just make things worse. Anyway, I'm supposed to be resigned. How hard it is to leave things in your hands, Lord! I want to meddle for his own good, but I keep feeling You draw me back.

And Aurelius was indeed leaving again. He didn't think that the old man would lose control to the extent of actually watching him depart. All the same, he felt compelled to move slowly, deliberately, as if preparing to confront a duty. He supposed that he should feel guilty, at least for the old man's sake, but he felt anything but that. His legs had an almost irresistible life of their own and he caught himself moving and accelerating in motion until he had to check himself with an effort.... The day is so lovely. Last time it rained and we could find no sensible reason to ride out together. I don't think that anyone actually would have asked us for a reason but it would have been just too awkward. Neither of us would have been comfortable with it.

If I get there a little earlier, we'll have more time. I can lunch on the ride. The old cook won't mind. But would Jimena laugh at me? She's the one who was raised in the country but I always seem to be the country bumpkin. Maybe Ram, Neppy, and I should have paid a little more attention to manners. I wonder if Neppy has found a girl yet? I wonder how many girls Ram has found just since I left? What am I all red and blushing about?

He could recall almost nothing of the path through the forest and fields but he was already upon the slope leading up to the great hall of the count. There was a bustle of hounds and more than two dozen mounts stamped and pawed in the clay before the palace door. He could make out the bailiff, Britto, wending his way through the group of warriors with a hooded hawk upon his wrist. The count doesn't have his own master of birds. It was going to be a big hunt for five or six of the warriors were edging or sheathing boar spears.

Just as Oro came up the count and Bishop Teodemiro emerged from the hall. Both wore the leather leggings and boots that mark the hunter of boars. They were smiling, obviously anticipating a day in the fields. Count Muño noticed Aurelius and motioned him off to one side of the group.

"I had entirely forgotten that you were supposed to put in your appearance today. You can see that my brother and I are headed out for a day of hunting. You could join us if you wish" Clearly the young man doesn't know what to say. From the look of his face I would say that he will go if I insist but he'll make damn poor company on a hunt. I think that my daughter has her hook in him about as far as it will go. Well, a love-sick puppy has its uses but running the field isn't one of them. I'd best find a way to let him off my own hook or the boy will come along with us out of sheer good manners. That would spoil everything.

"Still, it may be that we will be out for a day or two and that wouldn't do for your old faker, would it? He'd worry about you. Might even think that you were making a run for it and get all upset with you." Then, lowering his voice slightly, "I expect that you and my daughter will be taking a ride. It appears that the two of you have formed that habit. You do know, Aurelius, that she is the only child that I have left to me? I count on you to take care with her. Don't mistake me on that."

Was the count laughing at him? At both of them? He had the look of knowing about him and the young man found it embarrassing and at the same time offensive. But he was enormously relieved that the old tyrant was not going to press him to go along with them. He was also delighted that they were obviously just about to depart and that in a moment or two he would be free. Free for the whole rest of the day. He had to struggle to conceal his real feelings.

"I thank you for your offer, sir, but I am not very good at running the boar. I would like to do it sometime. Maybe the next time? And Jimena, your daughter, had intended to show me more of your country. She is very kind to me that way."

"Good God!" gasped the father under his breath. Could he be more obviously moonstruck? I think that I'd better talk to my daughter when I get back. She will be very good at prying him away from that looney old man but we need to be sure that he is what he says he is before we let this go any further. A little royal blood wouldn't hurt the family's position but I'd have no use for a traitor's bastard. The count nodded Oro his dismissal and rejoined the hunting party. It had been waiting on his signal and now began to move off with a great clatter, much shouting, and not a little laughter.

In turn, Aurelius had scarcely time to reach the kitchen before Jimena appeared. She was resplendent in a golden tunic worked with red and green thread in the likeness of an eagle. The bird's wings curled beneath her breasts and its neck and head thrust up between them. The ebony leather belt about her waist, by the limits that it set, served further to heighten the effect. The girl knew that the style of her garb was deliberately provocative but it had become more and more important to her to attract his admiration. Now, for that very reason, she strove to appear simple, relaxed.

"Oro, I have had the cook wrap some foods for us and we can take them along on our ride. That way we can have the entire day to ourselves. Is that all right?"

Without waiting on a reply she hurried on. "The extra time will let us reach a beautiful forest glen that we haven't yet visited. We can have ourselves a lunch in the fields just as my father and his friends are doing."

He could not remember exactly what he replied. She swept him up with her own enthusiasm and vitality which, in fact, mirrored his own. When they were together there developed an excitement which fed upon itself. But the horses had an easy time of it. The two were so intent upon their chatter that they rode deliberately and as close together as the trail permitted so as not to interrupt their happiness.

"You know, Oro, I think often that the reason you are so new, so innocent, must be because you never knew your mother. I think that as a little boy you must have lived alone in a secret world in your own mind. A mother would have drawn you out of that more. She would have taught you to be more aware of what other people around you are thinking. I like you just as you are but a mother's training would have made many things easier for you."

"But you told me, Jimena, that your mother died when you were no more than four years old. And you always know what to say, who needs to be flattered, who encouraged."

"Yes, my mother died in giving birth to the third of my brothers but ...."

"Three brothers?"

"For a time, yes. But a very brief time. That is why, perhaps, my father is so often hard, so often angry. My oldest brother I hardly knew. I was a little girl when he fell from a horse on a campaign in the south. My second one was closer to my age but died one winter from the breathing sickness—the one that makes people spit blood—when he was eight, I think. The last baby hardly lived a month after my mother's own death."

"So then you have grown up alone, too."

"Oh, Oro, a woman is never alone. A boy can grow up without women, in just the company of other boys, but a woman has many mothers. Every serving girl, and every cook, every mistress of my father's has had a hand in raising me. That is just the way that women are. In your palace, I suppose, every man felt that your education was your uncle's business. And the women would have been slow to meddle in such important matters. Royal matters always smell like intrigue!"

"I guess you're right. But I don't remember ever wanting any of the palace women to poke into my business. They were kind enough when I asked for something but, outside of that, I preferred to have my freedom. We used to have great games, Ram, and Neppy, and myself. We could go anywhere we wanted. Except for those times that we had to spend learning to handle weapons, and to track and read animal habits we had the whole day to ourselves. Well, that's not quite true. On Saturdays we had to sit with the priest and con our letters. We parsed some of the psalms, if you know what I mean. Sundays, of course, we attended mass with our uncle and after he would sometimes examine us on our Latin, particularly on the mass prayers."

"Oh, I quite understand what you mean. More than you think. I have some Latin myself. And I could sing you a psalm or two if I wanted. My father thought that I should be able to—though he can't himself. He says that the king is more monk than man."

She looked at him closely, anxiously. "Maybe I should not have said that?"

Oro smiled to reassure her. "Everyone else says it. Why not you?"

"And I can hunt too. You'll see. I took some of the baked sparrows that cook gave us for lunch myself, with a net. And I'm a fair shot with a bow, a light one anyway. And I can ride as well as you can. Here! Just over there. We're here."

The glade was a sort of natural amphitheater. The great granite boulders typical of the country formed an almost regular circle in whose central bowl a small spring bubbled crystalline. Yet a few yards away its entire flow sank mysteriously below the surface leaving not a trace even of mud. The firs that ringed the rocky edges rose more than twice a man's height before branching and their needle fall carpeted the entire space within.

They could have eaten easily from that surface without the cloak that Jimena had swirled into place by the spring. But Oro watched as the girl unloaded the pouch of foods.

She had seated herself back on her own legs with tunic drawn up slightly above her knees. Like a servant girl, yet with the air of a great lady too, he thought, she drew from the pouch one after the other, wineskin, bread, knife, onions, cheese wrapped in a wetted cloth, and tiny shells of hard-baked clay which she knocked, one against the other, and then pried the ruptured pieces away from the tiny bird baked within.

As she worked, he watched the deftness of her long fingers and the strength of her hands. She sliced through the breadwheel and divided its pieces. The onions became rings as he watched. Folding back the cloth with her free hand, she pared a bit of the yellow-gray substance ,goatcheese, between knife and thumb and nibbled it there with full lips. He was caught by the play of the sunlight as it pierced the breaks made by the wind stirring in the branches and fell over her hands and arms, lighting from time to time the reddish-golden down. In some confusion, he finally noticed that Jimena was watching him as he watched her. She was smiling.

"You're not hungry?" she asked. "It is very pretty the way that you sit and stare but we are going to eat, are we not?" As she said that, she blushed furiously.

It occurred to him that she was as nervous as he. "Yes. Sure. I'm starved." And he took the piece of cheese that she had extended to him.

They ate with the easy, unlimited appetite of the young. The warmth of the day, and then of the wine, made conversation flow naturally for a time.

"You say, Oro, that you enjoyed growing up with your cousins but I can guess that you were pretty lonely more than just once in a while. It shows in the kind of person you are now. You say that you had fun with them but you don't sound at all like them. You don't sound to me as if you wanted to be like them."

"Well, we had fights sometimes. Ram always had to be the leader, the one who picked the time or the game. Neppy? I guess sometimes he made me want to just go ahead and do something. Just to get it over and done. He always had a hundred different ways to do anything at all. He could talk forever. But I—we got over it. I think that we were just like everybody else."

"Except you. You were the one who went off by himself to dream, I'll bet. And so you turned out to be special, gentler and kinder than your cousins."

Oro was becoming slightly embarassed by her words but they were not unwelcome. He liked her implied preference for himself even if she had never met his cousins. Still, it did seem as though he should defend them, a little bit anyway. They were his buddies.

"Well, I don't know. We had good times. But you must have been lonely a lot of times. I mean, you lost your brothers—all of them."

"What I really missed was having a sister. The women were really kind to me. It may sound terrible but I didn't actually miss my mother very much. I mean after the first week or two. Girls always fight with their mothers. Especially when they get a little older and begin to think like women. Sometimes it's easier to talk with a woman who isn't part of the family. You know, that you can push off if they start to know too much about you.

"But a sister I would think that you could run with, just talk to, tell your dreams to because she couldn't betray them to anyone else because you had her dreams to hold as well. She would be somebody who could cry with you. Not somebody who would be too quick to try to tell you that everything is all right. We know, don't we, that things will be all right but we want to have our cry first.

"I know that I would have liked to have a sister but now it is too late. Now I think that I don't want a woman for a friend even. Not for a while. Maybe when I'm married and going to have a baby. Then might be nice."

She hesitated momentarily. "For now I am quite content—happy—just to have you for a friend, Oro. Just for now it is lovely to have you to talk to. I didn't think that I could share so much with a boy—man—but that's what I'm doing, isn't it?"

What should he say? Not something dumb. Dear God, not something dumb. Not again. Not this time.

"I think you are beautiful, Jimena. I think that you are the loveliest woman that I have ever known. It makes me happy all over just to sit and listen to you. I want to know everything about you." Why did I say that? It was too much. She'll think that I am a lunatic. She'll be frightened. That wasn't what we were talking about. Just what was in my mind. But I didn't have to come right out and say it. The way she's looking at me! She doesn't know what to say. What can we talk about now? I've spoiled it again!

I have to think of something to say! He's embarrassed himself and if I don't he may even run away and hide. I love him. Dear God, help me to think. Help me to let him know that it is all right. How I wanted him to say something like that. But what can we talk about now? "I think you are becoming a flatterer, Oro. You sound a little bit like the men in my father's court. But it was a beautiful thing to say." Oh my, look at his face. I've hurt his feelings. Stupid, stupid, stupid! Why can't I think of something to get us out of this?

"Look, Aurelius. Do you see that bluff over there? There is the most marvelous view of the country from the top of it. It is almost as beautiful as your compliment. Can we climb up and see it together? I would like that. Come on!"

The bluff, cliff actually, towered over the grove in which they had picnicked to a height of more than a hundred feet of granite face. But for all its forbidding front the approach to it that they took, from the rear, was a gentle and wooded slope.

A difficult climb would have been better, Jimena thought. It would have kept us busy with the ascent itself. As it is, we are both still nervous over what we said back there and we can't think of some other subject that is safe. The silence keeps growing between us and it is becoming enormous. I can feel my heart pounding in my breast and its pulse makes it impossible to think clearly. And Oro, poor thing, can't do any better. We just plod along, afraid to glance at one another for more than an instant. This whole day is turning out to be terrible. And I wanted it to be perfect.

Thank God, we've reached the top. "Oro, look! There in the west you can see the ocean itself. That thin line, almost silver. in the very farthest distance."

He could see it just faintly. With the sun now in the west the glare made it necessary to squint. He shaded his eyes with his palm. Out over the top of what looked to be, from this height, a continuous sea of green firs a hawk circled in a wide spiraling track. As he watched, it suddenly folded its wings and dropped like a stone to the level almost of the tree tops. Then the great wings unfolded again as it began to climb. Though he could not see for the distance surely it had made its kill. The stillness seemed suddenly more intense. The wind in the trees dropped away and left only the soft call of a dove and the faint murmur of bees. He felt as he had more than once when swimming under water. He was alone in the world that ignored him, that did not know his presence.

"Oro. Oro?" It was Jimena. She had touched his arm to get his attention and the contact jerked him back, taut and trembling, to their present. She was standing quite close. Close enough that he could catch the scent of her body. Her eyes were wide and a tiny vein beat in her throat.

"Oro, I have to ask you something. It is very bold but I need to know it. You don't have to answer if.... No! You do have to answer. Tell me now. How much does that old man with whom you live have power over you? Will you stay with him forever? Are you going to become a monk?"

The words tumbled from her with increasing speed. She had not removed her hand from his arm but she seemed unconscious of the fact.

"I don't know, Jimena. He tells me that I must. Sometimes, when I sit with him in watching, in some kind of prayer I suppose, there is this beautiful peace that creeps over me. I think that I see—I don't know what—just out there beyond me. It calls to me yet it does not speak. It is unutterably beautiful yet I cannot see it.

But other times my whole body aches. We sit for so long that I want to jump out of my skin itself. I want to scream until the sky splits. I want to run until I drop. But of course I don't. I just sit and think to myself how hungry I am. I remember the last meal that I had that was cooked and the last fruit I had that was sweet and I can hardly keeping from drooling at the memory. And I am altogether miserable because I feel that I am deceiving Alvitus. That I am acting a lie." She is staring at me. Her eyes are wet. What will I do if she weeps?

"Aurelius, listen to me." Her voice was husky, very deep, but it quavered as she began. "I want you to marry me. I want to be your wife. I want to carry your children. If you love me, you must leave that old man right away. He has some kind of magic. I can see that from what you tell me. But that is for him. God has called him. But God has sent you to me. I am sure of that. I felt something special from the very first time we met. Without you I shall die."

The words had, finally, rushed from her in a torrent. Oro drew her to him. He could feel her shake along the whole length of his body.

"I love you, Jimena. You are my soul. You are my life."

His hands went beneath her tunic. Her arms were about his shoulders. He was dizzy with her scent. He fumbled awkwardly with her breech-clout. Jimena did not move to resist him but instead pressed her breasts more closely against his chest. He was afire with their roundness. Then he found the pin and her undergarment slipped free. Aurelius bent yet more towards her and the girl pressed his head against her breasts. His hands slid up behind her buttocks and on to the wonderful smooth softness of her back.

Then, without warning his whole body was in spasm. He fought to control it but he could not. He was helpless in the grip of his own passion. He ground his face against Jimena's breasts and groaned in despair.

"Wait! Wait for me! Stop for a minute!"

Oh God. Oh God. I'm shrieking. My whole body is aflame. I could kill him. And I'm trying to. I'm pounding on his head with my fists. If I could get at his face I'd claw it bloody. He had no right to do that without me—before I was ready. It is all spoiled. It was our minute and he couldn't manage to do it properly.

Jimena was dimly conscious of her own voice, loud and shrill. "You stupid, stupid boy! You think you know everything but you don't even understand how a man must act with a woman. You soil yourself with your own seed and it runs down on the ground and nothing, nothing is left for me. I wanted you to make love to me forever and you couldn't even wait for me."

Now she was pushing him, dazed, away from her. Pushing and hammering at his face as he sat motionless, on his heels now. She could hear her own voice as it ranted on. Saying things she did not mean, even in her frustration. Saying things that would wound and hurt and make life impossible between them. She felt as though she were bleeding to death and yet she could not stop.

"I hate you! No, don't touch me—ever! You sit there with that dumb expression! You had your satisfaction! You took it for yourself alone and left me racked and dry! Selfish and stupid! I will never see you again!"

Oh God! God forgive me! Forgive me, Aurelius! But whirling in a fury she snatched her loincloth from the ground. Her hand closed over the open clasp and it punctured her index finger. Sobbing with humiliation, and rage, and now with pain Jimena fled down the forest path. She did not stop until she reached her pony which she mounted in an instant. Cloak, wineskin, foodpouch all forgotten she rode furiously off, tears continuing to stream down her face.

Aurelius sat where she had left him. The day continued placid about him but his mind raced. For long he did not move from that spot, staring at the dirt before his face, but later he could not recall what he had thought.

Afterward he descended to that glade in the firs and numbly gathered up the reminders of the day. When he reached the palace of Jimena's father the place had an air of desertion. Jimena was nowhere and he would have been terrified to encounter her. Not even a groom was to be seen. He tethered his mount as close to the barn as he cared to go. At the kitchen he left Jimena's cloak and the rest of the foodstuffs. The old cook looked at him curiously but she said nothing. Nevertheless, he could feel the color swarm in his face and, retrieving his bow and quiver, he departed without a word to her. It was over—finished. That thought ran like a bardic refrain through his mind as he took up the long road home.

# Chapter Fourteen

I wish he would stop talking. I really wish the boy would just be silent. For a time there he seemed to be fairly happy, content. I thought that he would never stop chattering then. For the past two weeks he has been as sad as I've ever seen him and he still goes on and on. If you had to send me a companion, Lord, couldn't you have sent me a quiet one?

"Don't turn away from me, Alvitus. You're the one who told me that I was sent to you here by the Lord. So you're the one that has to help me."

"And I told you, Oro, that if you are going to get any answers they will come from the Lord, not from me. I know as little about what we're doing here as you do."

"That's not true and you know it. You're hiding behind your precious God. You've already told me, in part anyway, how you came to be here. Well, I came to be here in more or less the same way. So you could help me with that much of it. At least with the beginning of things."

"So you think, boy, that we are the same. That you have walked my road, in my steps? Come back in thirty years and we will measure that out again."

"In part, Alvitus, in part. You know what I mean. You're here because you ran away from the world. Because you could not stand what people were doing to one another.

What you were doing to them. You ran away from them and from yourself—and then you found something—someone. Isn't that what you told me?"

"That was the start of it, Aurelius, yes. But it was only the start of it. And you are too young to know the full horror of what we human beings are like. You haven't seen men torture and kill one another in a drunken stupor—or even just because they're bored. You...."

"I've seen enough. I saw an old man stabbed to death in front of his own daughter! And I saw men hunt another man. Tie him up and lead him about like an animal. And for money. Just for money. They didn't even hate him. He might as well not have been there. He wasn't there, as far as they were concerned. They paid no more attention to him than you would if you were leading a sheep to the butcher. Less. He had become no more than human meat to them just because they had caught him.

And then I saw an old lady naked and without shame. She had probably saved my life. She nursed me when I was sick, kept me warm and fed me. Her husband had found me unconscious and next to dead on the trail in the mountains. They were both kind to me. But she was so desperate for a little happiness, a little pleasure, that she was ready to betray the old man for an hour or so of being pawed by or pawing a young boy who found her disgusting and ran from her as fast as he could get away. She had no pride left, nor any trace of dignity.

So that's how I came here. I'm a runaway, a fugitive, just like you yourself. We're both hiding out together."

The older man's eyes flashed and his words tumbled out one upon the other.

"No, you are not just like me! We are different enough, you and I. You are pathetic, Aurelius. You don't have the courage to give up that muck. You keep looking back, thinking that perhaps it will change. That it will be different next time. You've stepped just outside of the house but you can't bring yourself to close the door behind you. You don't have the courage, either, to stike out on the new path. You want someone to take you by the hand and lead. You want playmates. Christ's blood! They betrayed you before and you want to take them along for company so that they can betray you again. Use your head, boy!"

Now it was the younger man who lashed out. His arms were wrapped around his chest. He squeezed himself in his intensity and rocked slightly back and forth.

"You don't understand, Alvitus. You don't even try. You're afraid to try. For weeks you've been busy—eager—to keep me here. All this time you tell me that I have been sent to be your helper in some terrible, important thing that is just about to happen. But it hasn't happened has it? No! And yet you keep on telling me that our task is to wait patiently, to pray, to listen.

Well, I have waited and I have prayed and I have listened. And no one has come. And no one has heard my prayers. They bounce off the inside of my head. No one hears them except me and I can't remember them from one minute to the next. And every time I stop mumbling to myself and listen the silence deafens me. It sucks me dry! The silence gets inside me and turns my bones to dust. I can't remember joy. I can't hear the birds sing. I can't smell the poppies. I am lost and still no one comes. I'm alone and I'm afraid of being left alone.

So I ask you old man. I ask the one who tells me what it is that I am expected to do and why I have been sent to this place of torture. If I am supposed to be here, why is it that I want desperately to be somewhere else—anywhere else?

Shouldn't I at least be happy—or satisfied even—to be here? Does your God want only unhappy servants? Am I a slave? Why doesn't He speak to me? He spoke to you."

The holy man's visage softened almost imperceptibly. Almost inaudibly he sighed. What am I supposed to tell him? What is there to tell? His questions are just the ones I asked myself—still do sometimes—and I've never gotten an answer. But it must be hard at his age to do without answers. I don't remember now much of what it was like to be that young. Did You really send him here? Or am I just creating a mission for him to soothe my own loneliness? Lord, I say that I did not ask for someone to help in this strange call You have fashioned for me but perhaps I did—really. Forgive me for serving You! Teach me to sit still!

Alvitus spoke so quietly as to be scarcely audible. "I find myself telling you the same thing over and over, Oro. I have no other words for you. You journeyed here from Oviedo and you almost died in making the trip. Did you know who you would meet here? Could you have guessed at the start that all those things of which you have told me would have happened to you? If you had known, would you still have made the trip? What now, in your own mind, is the important thing—that you have arrived here or that you did make the journey?

"I had nothing to do with it, you know. I did not send for you. I did not even pray that you would be sent. You just stumbled in here, green, and skinny, and obviously lost and alone. What happened to me then I do not honestly understand. No one spoke to me. It doesn't happen so. Words are not part of it. Our words are just babbling, noise and no more, and no words come from His side. But I knew that you had been sent! When I tell you that I do not lie. In the very moment that you appeared out of the forest, I knew that your arrival was no accident, no chance, neither trick nor trial. Since then I have been waiting—like you—to discover the reason why you have been sent to me. I cannot tell you what I do not know myself.

"Look, Aurelius. This is another journey that you have begun. You didn't ask for it, did you? But then you didn't ask to be exiled from Oviedo either, did you? Both things have just happened to you. Did you know where you were going then—I mean really? Did you know who you were going to meet and how you were going to get there? All you had was the name of someone you had never met before. Is this so different? You are called to be a man and it frightens you. But what choice do you have?

Yes, you are going to be lonely, more alone than you have ever been in your life. So tighten up your guts and get on with it. So you are hungry? Who isn't? So you are lost? Who isn't? Every child thinks that they are special. But they all grow up -if they're lucky—and find out that they are just like everyone else. Then maybe they begin to be honest with themselves. You need to do that.

"You say that you have had no answer at all? Yet you have stayed. Is that just because you feel sorry for a crazy old man sitting alone facing a forest at the edge of the world? I don't think so. I think that you have felt something here. I think you have found the beginning of a trail. But you are afraid to follow it because you don't know where it leads. Neither do I! It is your trail! But it is there and you know that it is there. All you have to do is put your head down and follow it. Forget the rest! Forget everything else! You have to do this! You will never be the same if you do not! Don't 'kick against the goad,' Aurelius. None of us choose our own destiny. Yet when it is shown us, we have only the choice to follow along it."

As he finished speaking his words seemed to drain the breath and blood out of the holy man. His body appeared to shrink beneath his cloak and he himself to become scarcely more than a heap of ragged clothing piled upon the ground. Suddenly Alvitus had gone away somewhere.

He's grieving Aurelius thought. He's grieving for me! The old man actually wants to help me and he is wrapped in sorrow because he can find no way. The young man could feel the sting of tears starting in his eyes. Since he had left his uncle in Oviedo he had missed the certainty that some strong masculine presence valued him and sought to keep him from harm. He had missed that sort of paternal care without even becoming conscious of his need for it. And now he felt its presence again in the gruff, difficult old hermit. It didn't even matter that it was useless, couldn't help him really.

No, that wasn't true. He felt acutely guilty of a sudden. Perhaps the old man could help him but he had not told Alvitus the truth. Not all of it anyway. About Jimena he had not said a thing. Possibly the hermit could not help him just because he did not know the whole truth. Because I have deliberately kept the full truth from him. He thinks that I have stayed with him because I have come to share a little bit of his vision of the holy. He does not understand that I have remained here, at least in part, because of her. This calling gave me an excuse for remaining near her but at the same time allowed me time apart from her to try to understand what it was that I was coming to feel and what I would have to do.

But that is over now. We are finished, Jimena and I. I humiliated her and she hates me for it. So why can't I now tell Alvitus the full truth about my feelings? I am afraid that he will despise me for deceiving him. No! I'm more afraid that he would laugh at me. Not out loud, of course, but he often finds me amusing in his damn superior, old man's sort of way. All the same I'm afraid that he would laugh and I don't think that I could forgive him for that. I'd rather do without his help than to tell him the truth about Jimena and me.

Jesus! He felt his heart constrict at the thought of her. A vision of green eyes and auburn tresses came, unbidden to his mind's eye, and a helpless rage filled him. It was not fair! It was not fair! He hadn't meant.... What? He had wanted to, God knows. And she had half allowed him! And then he had spoiled it all! He had made a fool of himself and had embarrassed her beyond speaking. How could he describe any of that to the hermit who had become his father?

But there was no way to tell Alvitus anything. The man had disappeared, shrunk into himself, shrunk into his clothes. Oro had the eerie feeling that if he were to reach out and touch that pile of clothes that they would collapse into emptiness under his hand.

Alvitus continued to fall. He had plunged away from Oro suddenly and without warning. How long have I been falling? The wind rushing past my nostrils sucks the breath out of my body. The surface is gone and I cannot touch the sides. I can feel them coming together yet I cannot touch them. The place into which I am hurtling is beoming narrower and narrower as I fall and yet I cannot touch, cannot grasp, anything. It isn't dark! I'm not losing the sun! But still I cannot see anything. I'm falling so fast that the wind is pulling tears to my eyes and I am blinded by my own fluids.

I think that my chest is collapsing. The air is so heavy that it presses my lungs against my heart. I'm falling so fast that my stomach is being forced up against them both. The wind flowing over me is warping me, folding me, turning me in on myself. There is nothing left of me—nothing but a little round ball, floating in the air.

Floating in the air! And spinning! I've ceased to fall. I've arrived somewhere! And yet, there is nothing! The air is so marvelously bright and has no end. It goes on and on. I can see forever but there is nothing there. No earth, no sky, no trees, no sound! But although I cannot grab anything, I cannot even reach out of myself, I am....somewhere. A somewhere that is nowhere? I'm resting on nothing. No, I'm floating on nothing. And I'm spinning in the middle of....nothing.

No, no, not nothing! Those are branches! But they're not! They're roots. Roots of salt? Roots of crystal? Roots of crystal that twine and entwine. They too float on this marvelous air, and wave and flutter like fronds, like branches, like seaweed perhaps. And deep within them they caress and shelter a temple of shell. A house of mother of pearl all surrounded with columns and glistening with seafoam.

But the roots are not really supporting, not really enfolding the temple. They are pressing on it. They are prying at it. Those crystal fingers are tearing and wrenching at the columns -at the very building blocks themselves! The entire structure is disintegrating and I can hear it scream. High and clear, it is like a fox being torn apart by dogs. Like a woman in labor! It hurts the ears and there is no refuge from it.

The walls are crumbling, blocks and groups of blocks rushing outward. Rushing towards me! They hurtle past me but I am a little ball turning in the air and they cannot touch me. I feel the wind stirred by their passage but they do not strike. And still the restless crystal fronds seek and pry, and tear, and the temple falls upon itself and pours out its golden contents which bounce upon the surface of the air and strike one against the other with a sound like gongs and church bells and solitary song heard in the distance. They are little golden coins, full of music, that jostle and dance, and play upon the currents of the air, coming always closer.

But they are not little coins. The closer they get the more I can see that they are like shields, like the great circular shields a man carries into battle only carved and embossed and chased in wonderful shapes. Yet they are soft gold, and their shapes writhe and bend and twist so that they cease altogether to be coins or shields and seem to become more like sticks, like tree branches—no, like bones! They are bones, the bones of a dead giant turning in the air and raining down on me! I am struck. I am flung! I ....! I....! I....!

A shadow had fallen upon them both, upon Oro and himself. I am here! Back! I have never left. But it has begun! The time will not be long now. All these months and now it starts! I should be glad but I feel instead as though I might soil myself. My bowels are loose inside of me and my heart batters against my rib cage. My God, help me when I fall into your hands! Help us both! Save the boy!

"My Lord Aurelius, Count Muño has sent me to escort you back to the palace. You have neglected your usual visits for two weeks now and my master is concerned about you."

It was Britto. The bailiff sat on one horse and led another already saddled. He was alone—and his spear was in its sheath and his bow unstrung. Oro had feared that perhaps they might send soldiers and trackers after him. But it was only the surly bailiff and the count had sent him a horse as well.

"Aurelius cannot go with you. He is needed here now."

It was Alvitus who had spoken. The bailiff glowered at

him, startled that he should interfere. Surprised that the dour old hermit should have spoken to anyone.

"Mind your mouth, old man, this is the count's business. Meddle in it and you will bleed for it."

"Ah, you great, animated turd! Never have I seen cow shit riding a pony! I have pulled better men than you off real horses, not a sorry nag like that, and crushed their skulls with a rock. I will do the same favor for you if you continue to plague us."

Britto was struck almost dumb. Like most big men entrusted with a little authority he was unaccustomed to being opposed. This bearded little old splinter of a man looked ready to fly up off the ground and attack him. He was too surprised to speak. In his anger the bailiff felt the temptation to spear him like a toad. But he knew that the count would never forgive him. Actually Count Muño might well be glad to have the old fake dead, so long as it was by someone else's hand. But that would not stop his master from playing at a show of indignation and finding a particularly unpleasant way for him to die.

The danger was clear to Oro. He did not understand the sudden high emotion of his mentor but, whatever its cause, it could get the hermit killed. He intervened without hesitating.

"Well, now that you're here, Britto, you can see that I have not run away. I am still keeping my bargain with your master. You can go back and tell him that. In a few days I can follow along."

The big bailiff actually seemed relieved that he had spoken. But nevertheless his attitude continued both stubborn and churlish as he now addressed himself to Aurelius.

"All well and good for you, young sir, but I have my

orders from the count. He said to bring you back with me. It would cost me stripes to take back the kind of message you suggest."

"But why must the count see me just now? What is so important all of a sudden that he sends you to find me? Sends you with a horse besides."

The thought had come to him all of a sudden that it was Jimena. That this summons was about the count's daughter. Had someone spied upon them? He could not believe that she would have complained. Or had her pain turned to rage and vengeance? Now he did not want a reply to the question just out of his mouth. He went limp with relief at the bailiff's response.

"I don't know, sir. Count Muño does not often tell me such things. He just tells me what I must do and I do it."

As the bailiff finished he glanced and glowered at Alvitus. The hermit, who had been regarding him all the while, glared back.

"Well go tell your lord and master that Aurelius is busy with the work of God. That's a higher authority than old Muño or even his brother, Teodemiro the bishop. There is going to be such a work done here that the whole world will be set on end. And not all of the count's warriors can prevent that, much less one moth-eaten, evil-smelling, wine-swilling thief of a bailiff.

"All of you are going to learn for the first time what your God is really like. You'll see his power and you will run like women. Your bones will turn to water and your swords will turn to butter.

"Aurelius is going to be a part of that. God plans it for him and neither count nor bishop had better interfere. They will bleed for it, not me. Go back to your master and tell him to tremble.Tell him to repent if he remembers what the word means. Tell him to hurry for the last time is upon him."

Britto could do no more than gape. Sure the old man was crazy but no one had heard such madness as this from him before now. He could feel his flesh creep upon his arms and neck.

Aurelius too reeled at the hermit's words. Alvitus had never talked of the end, the thing, as imminent up till now. When had he gotten his message? Moments ago, it seemed, they had been talking as though the path was long, weary. The old man had tried to brace him for the long journey. Now he spoke of it being upon them! He wished, suddenly, to get away. The old man had become strange, menacing. His foster father had disappeared and his place had been taken by a warlock, a sorcerer!

"Perhaps it is better that I answer the count's summons, Alvitus."

The holy man jerked around to regard him—looked at him in unbelief. Oro hurried on. Something terrible was about to happen here. At the very least the death of Britto or maybe even of Alvitus. He had to prevent that. The hermit had to let him go. He wanted to go.

"You told me that we did not know, would not know the path. That it would be wholly the work of the Lord. Well, perhaps the summons from the count is part of it. You are sure now that something is coming to a head. I hear you say it. Well, is it strange then that just now—just this moment—a call comes for me that we never expected? Is it part of the plan. Shouldn't I answer it and see."

The boy is frightened. Why not? I'm shaking all over. I could jump out of my skin. But I had hoped that he would stay—that he would want to stay. I don't want to suffer this alone. But aloud he only said, "That blood-sodden old sinner as God's instrument. Even I would find it difficult to credit such a thing as that. As well tell me that our noble Britto here is a secret philospher. You turn my own words against me, Oro. Have you heard that one does well not to trust the Devil even if he quotes Scripture?

Even so, what you suggest is just barely possible. You can go. But swear that you will return! You cannot escape your path, boy. I tremble for you if you even attempt that. And pray that you are not rejected for this desertion. Go and see your precious count but when he has worked his corruption, come back to me. And hurry, boy, hurry. There is not much time. There may be none. I will keep you in my mind as best I can but I can promise you nothing. If you are not here when He strikes you have lost everything. God help you then!"

But Oro was already upon his feet. There seemed no need to take anything. Britto, relieved at the prospect of leaving this place of demons, was proffering him the reins of the second horse. Thrusting them upon him. In the back of his mind, Oro thought that by taking nothing of his belongings the old man would be doubly reassured of his return. He blushed for his own dishonesty at that thought. Would Alvitus too sense his terrible falseness? Would he come back? He was not sure that he could—that he could make himself return or that he would even try.

He took the reins and swung hurriedly into the saddle.

"I'll be back, Alvitus. I'll be back soon."

# Chapter Fifteen

So this is how power feels. I think that I like it. This leopard skin that they've used to drape my chair must have come up from Africa across the straits. In Córboba it cost dear enough and constituted a major bribe when they sent it north for Count Muño. The count and his brother the bishop are seated on mere bearskin. And my head is higher than theirs too, by just a little bit. But I can't take too obvious notice of it. I don't want to make permanent enemies of either of them.

"So you understand, my Lord Aurelius, that we had to be sure. Your story and appearance were unusual, as you must realize. But as soon as King Alfonso sent word that you were indeed his cousin, we had to invite you so that we might properly recognize you and prepare for the king's arrival. He has not visited Galicia for five years now but he will probably be hard on the heels of our ambassadors. It will take some time to prepare a proper welcome."

The count hesitated and then glanced at his brother, who seemed just perceptibly to nod assent.

"You will be interested, Lord Aurelius, to learn that the king has sent word as well that Count Ordoño is dead. Some kind of a—hunting accident."

There was an awkward pause when Oro offered no comment to this information. It seemed to him that he would need to know the mind of his uncle before sharing court gossip and intrigue with these two. Besides, he owed them little or nothing. Bishop Teodemiro broke the growing silence.

"We had thought, subject to your wishes of course, that it would be best to receive the king in Iria Flavia. The episcopal palace there is somewhat more grand, somewhat more spacious, than this forest stronghold of my brother's. In any event, we thought that the king would welcome a mass in the cathedral there. His majesty is the most truly Christian king that we have had, ever perhaps, and takes an intelligent interest in the sacramental life."

More maybe, thought Oro, than do you. But aloud he merely said, "I am sure, your excellency, that you and the count your brother will know much more about how these things are best arranged than would I. I will leave it completely in your hands."

"Well then," Count Muño interjected, "We need two or three days to prepare the household for the move down to the coast and, most importantly, we have to make proper arrangements for your own comfort and service. You don't appear to have brought anything much with you. Would you like me to send Britto to collect whatever you might have left behind that we cannot better replace?"

Oro was tempted. That would be a clean break and would avoid the embarrassment of having to confront Alvitus over his desertion. He did not want to return. The hair on his neck prickled when he thought of what might be taking place there, even now. Still, the holy man had become a sort of father and the young man knew that he could not simply run away. In any event, he now had the impending visit of King Alfonso as an excuse for his return once again to the palace of the count—though admittedly that might not impress the hermit very much.

"I can just as easily attend to that business myself. No need to trouble your bailiff further. If I might have the use of one of your horses?

The count could not entirely suppress the frown that glided across his features. His eyes went to his brother. Then he spoke. "You can understand I hope, Lord Aurelius, what trouble this crazy old man can make for us. The people take him half-seriously already. But now that your real identity is known the problem is compounded. Any association with him on your part from now on will be interpreted by them as a sign of the royal favor itself. Of course, the confusion and ignorance of the peasants by itself is easily controlled but there are elements just now among the warriors throughout the territory who would be glad of an excuse to use that confusion against our authority.

"Let the bailiff reclaim your possessions. That in itself would begin to let the peasants understand that your stay there was simply a device to avoid recognition."

Oro felt himself flush. The count was being polite enough.... but he will manipulate me as much as he can. And he has no idea of what Alvitus is. Quite intentionally, the young man let a note of harshness creep into his reply.

"We—you—are going to have to deal with the man whether you care to or not. He is more, much more, than just a 'crazy old man.' He's a seer, a prophet perhaps. While I had my doubts for a long time, I have come now to understand that he genuinely possesses some kind of vision."

"All the more dangerous then." Bishop Teodemiro broke in. "He may be possessed. He may be a heretic. There may be magic at work. I understand that he has just begun to predict a great and imminent cataclysm. A little more encouragement and there will be hysteria among the ignorant."

Oro was puzzled then until he recalled that, just after his arrival, he had seen the bailiff, Britto, in earnest conversation with the bishop. Damn! His mentor was in greater danger than he knew.

"My lord bishop should realize that so far he has but the word of an "ignorant peasant" for that. I am not sure myself precisely what Alvitus meant. But if some miracle of sorts does happen, what can we do but accept it? We can hardly prevent it. We can hardly reject it. And if, after a time, nothing happens, he will lose credit with the people soon enough."

"You are very young, Lord Aurelius." Bishop Teodemiro was barely able to maintain the facade of deference. His face had turned ruddy and his hands had clenched in his lap.

"This sort of meddler with the world of the supernatural has a thousand excuses. He will extend the date. He will allege a new revelation. And we are by no means helpless in the face of signs and wonders. This sort of thing can be diabolic rather than divine. We have tests for such."

Oro smarted under the tone, and the logic as well, of the prelate. He was himself uncertain. He did not understand Alvitus. Certainly he was convinced that the old man was good, holy even. But was he sane, completely sane? He had had doubts himself more than once. Nevertheless, he feared danger in the talk of witchcraft and devils.

"Tests of that sort are better left to God himself, bishop! You and I should not meddle with what we don't understand."

"What you do not understand, young man! I have some knowledge of the world of the supernatural and the king, your uncle, will realize that if you do not. Those who begin by pleading ignorance should stay clear of matters like this."

The count was surprised that his brother had lost control of himself to such an extent as this. He intervened to prevent what could only be an open and a damaging quarrel. One which would have no resolution here anyway. "You are right, brother, that in this business the king will have a great interest. I'm sure that the Lord Aurelius knows and appreciates that as well. Let us hope that the danger can simply be hushed, postponed until the king himself arrives."

Then, to Oro, the count spoke in a less peremptory, reasonable tenor. "All that we ask, for the present, Lord Aurelius, is that you be as discreet as possible. If you wish to return to make your goodbyes, do it as quietly and briefly as you can. By night would be preferable. And, of course, you have the use of whatever of our mounts as suits you best. In fact, you may have whatever one you prefer as a gift from my brother and I. I will let Britto know of it.

"In the meantime, you should have garments more proper for a cousin of the king. For this I have already given orders. You know, I believe, the hut where our seamstress keeps our wardrobe. While we begin on the other arrangements for the visit of the king, you yourself might pick out there what you find pleasing and let us know thereafter what more you might require."

Oro understood that he was being bundled off politely. The count's main interest was to forestall an open quarrel. But he, himself, could see no quick solution. He was content to avoid more talk about Alvitus for now and so was happy to fall in with the count's device. He thanked the two brothers for their courtesy, rose, and left them to what, he was sure, would be some further, heated argument.

At the seamstress' hut the old lady was not to be seen.

There seemed to be no one about. Tentatively, he looked into the dim interior.

"Jimena!"

"My Lord Aurelius. My father commanded that I should assist you in choosing.... No, that is a lie. I asked my father if I could help you select clothing befitting a man of the royal house. I wanted this chance to apologize, to tell you...."

He placed his forefinger to her lips.

"Not 'My Lord Aurelius,' Jimena. Not even Aurelius. Oro, if you will have me. Can you ever forgive me for my stupidity, for my incredible clumsiness? I have come to love you and you have stolen my senses. I cannot control myself properly in your presence."

He stopped. He dared not believe. But her eyes were wet. She kissed his finger lightly. Then she came into his arms, trembling against him.

"Oh, Oro, can we begin over? It was all so lovely and I didn't understand how to keep it so. It was for me to arrange and I only partly knew how that must be. But I do love you. I will be your wife. Only say that you still want me." She held him with some fierceness even as she shook almost uncontrollably.

"I want to marry you, Jimena, more than anything else in this world."

At this the young woman pushed back a bit and surveyed him intently for a moment. Then, for the first time, she smiled. He felt that he would dissolve with relief.

"I have already chosen most of the things that I believe you will need and that will be suitable. They are there on that chest. Do you want to examine them and see if you like them?"

"No. I simply want to look at you again. I want to be sure that you are really smiling at me."

"Then, can we walk to the top of the rise behind the palace? Would you like that?"

"Yes."

He was afraid to venture more. It proved unnecessary. Jimena had his hand almost before he spoke and led him from the hut into the midday sun. A faint path rose into the fir wood that crowned the slight hill.

"Will you go back to your holy man? I know that my father and his brother were going to try whatever they could to dissuade you from that. Poor dears! They are at a loss how to handle you since it now seems that you boast the royal lineage."

"Yes, I will be going back but only for a little while—to collect my bow and quiver and a few other things. Your father is giving me a horse and I will ride back this evening. But I will soon be back here with you."

Jimena did not respond and a sudden pall seemed to have fallen over them. He tried to make light of it.

"Do you share your father's concern that old Alvitus will corrupt the locals?"

She appeared not to have heard him.

"I come up here when I wish to be alone for a time. I am the daughter of a count and so my father has forbidden anyone at all to trespass up here. And I have never brought anyone else here. Except for you now, I share it only with the birds and some small woods animals."

Well within the wood, they had reached a clearing and a pool of surprising dimension. He would have thought that the hill would hardly have provided a spring of the size necessary to feed it.

Over her shoulder Jimena asked suddenly, "Can you swim, Oro?"

"Yes. Not well, I guess, but I can swim some."

"Then swim with me!"

While he stood transfixed, Jimena cast the cloak that she had carried up from the wardrobe hut on the bed of needles. Another swift motion drew the hem of her tunic up over her shoulders and head. Then her nakedness flashed past him and vanished smoothly into the waters. For a long moment he was left staring at the widening ripples. Awkwardly he tugged off his own tunic, discarded his breechclout, and entered the pool in his turn.

Oro was a plodder in the water. He pulled strongly with his shoulders and kicked manfully if unevenly with his legs but it was heavy going for him. The water boiled in his wake and the small creatures native to the pool gave him wide berth. From side to side he went, puffing and hauling, but competently if not gracefully. Jimena, on the other hand, was an otter, a seal, a trout. Almost without a ripple she slid and glistened under and on the surface. She dived beneath him and swam around him. At his side at one minute, the next she was at the far extremity of the little water course. If another person had made such playful sport of him it would have been maddening.

Then, he became aware that she was gone. Looking up Oro found that she had left the pool and taken refuge on the cloak. Once again he thrashed his way back to the bank and hauled himself out.

Jimena had seated herself on the cloak and was combing out her hair, dark red now with the water, and reaching almost to her waist in its freedom from restraint of ribbon or comb. She had thrown a corner of the cloak across her loins but had disdained to reclaim her tunic. Oro was not at all sure what to do with his own. He had retrieved it from the pine needles before he noticed that Jimena had not donned hers. Now he held it awkwardly before him. He was painfully conscious that once he had left the cold waters of the pool he quickly had become fully extended.

The play of Jimena's young muscles, as she combed, raised and released her breasts and the blue veins shone dully beneath the creamy white texture of her flesh. Her nipples stood, reddish-brown, hard upon that surface. Oro was aware that she was behaving quite purposefully and deliberately. At the same time that Jimena was busy with the rearranging of her hair she was regarding him with a look that was at once frank and tense.

"Come sit, Oro, here before me. He did, somewhat clumsily for he still had not decided what he should do with the tunic clasped in his hands, or with his hands or, in fact, with his person. Finally he settled with the damn tunic in his lap and the young woman continued. She spoke a challenge.

"Do you think that I am a wanton, Oro?"

"I think that you are the most beautiful woman that I have ever seen."

"The sort of woman that you would marry? A woman whom you would marry against the wishes, if need be of the king, your uncle? Am I the woman whom you would marry in spite of the plans for you of Alvitus, your holy man and mentor?"

"Jimena, I will find a way. We will find a way. My uncle will probably decide on my cousin Ramiro as his successor anyway. Ram is harder than I am and older as well. So my marriage will be less important than his for the king's purposes. Alvitus thinks that I am destined to be a hermit like him but he doesn't know everything either. He thinks that I was guided here by God to be his assistant but I think that God sent me here to find you. I am slow, and sometimes I think stupid, but there is no one in this world who matters to me as much as you do. I want to be your husband, to share our lives forever."

"Then we can seal that love now, Oro. Don't be nervous. I know little more of this than you do. I have never let another man touch me, as you will discover for yourself in a moment or two. I know only what the gossip of old women tells. We can learn together. They say that to control yourself long enough to enter me you need to concentrate on breathing deeply and to be as little conscious of your own feelings as you can. And you need to fasten your eyes on mine and on my face.

So come to me now, my beloved."

Jimena had put down the comb and tossed back her hair. Now she turned back the corner of the cloak and motioned Oro forward, making a space for him between her legs.

His chest heaving, he put aside his tunic and knelt, then leaned towards her. Her hands reached out for his face and drew him forward upon her. She reclined backward slowly and bent her knees as he found himself in her embrace.

Dear God, help us to do this properly! Poor Oro has humiliated himself once already. If just this once.... Thank God! He has found me. I can feel him pushing, entering. There, there is the tearing, the pain that the old women told me to expect! Such a little though! And now, ah God, now he throbs inside of me! It is done!

"Oh Oro, my beloved, my sweetness. Tell me you love me. Tell me that you will love me forever."

Her hands roved across his back, down his buttocks, up his sides once again to his face, his neck, his hair. She kissed his lips, his cheeks, his ears, his eyes. The comfort of it filled her and gentled her and quieted her at last.

Aurelius who had been unable to do more for a time than gasp, whose throat was dry, feared that he would merely croak if he attempted to speak, only held her tightly and wondered at her warmth, her softness, the smoothness of her being. After a bit he moved gently from atop her and the two lay side by side, just touching, eyes closed, in the silence of content. A long, languid silence ensued while they both savored their rest and the completeness of their peace. Finally, it was Jimena who broke the spell.

"You could have commanded me, you know."

"What?"

He opened his eyes to see his love, raised on one elbow, regarding him closely.

"You are of royal lineage. You could have commanded the service of my body. If I am not mistaken that is what your cousin Ram would have done if he were you."

He was shocked at the idea but he could see that Jimena was serious. Sadly, he thought, she is probably right. Ram is like that. Has probably done just that more than once. He's a fool!

"No, I could not. What would I have obtained that way? What I might take—but I wanted only what you could give. And you have given all this, your self and body," he touched her breast gently, "simply because you love me. No king has so much."

Her eyes brimmed with tears. He means that just as he says. He is so good! So gentle of spirit it is a wonder that he has survived in this world for so long without me. But I will care for him. I will make him strong. I can teach him who his enemies are. And our children will move him to provide against them.

Her thoughts made Jimena almost dizzy with happiness, revived her passion. She was free now to indulge it, sure of its fruition. She began to stroke his body, lightly, then strongly, finally fiercely, restoring his strength bit by bit.

Now she bestrode him. Dipping she drew her nipples across his breast. Responding, he caressed them. He ran his hands along her sides and down into the softness of her thighs, lifting and flexing her.

"Come! Come now, beloved! Take me forever! Make me wholly your own!"

In answer to her throaty pleas, Oro began to thrust more and more strongly into her. They pressed urgently together as their blood raced and their bodies took on a sensate life of their own.

"Oh, dear God, how I love you! You fill me with meaning! I shall never live again without you. You have become my purpose and my existence! Hold me! Hold me! Hold me!"

After a time, exhausted, they slept, still couched in one another's arms. And the doves murmured to one another among the trees. The bees droned on the soft air of the afternoon. Somewhere close the brook emerged from the pond and tinkled off among the stones.

The first cool breath of approaching evening on his body awoke Aurelius and with one arm he drew part of the cloak over them. Jimena muttered sleepily and ducked her head away from the slanting light and against his chest.

"Truly we are married now. I will have to talk of it with my uncle as soon as he arrives. He will be angry, very angry, that we have gone so far without his permission but it is done. He will have to accept. I am determined.

"Perhaps we can convince your uncle, the bishop, to marry us in church. But before that there is your father. What will he say? Will you speak to him first or should I?"

From against his chest there now came the high, merry laughter of his wife, of Jimena.

"Oh Oro. There will be no trouble at all with my father. Don't you realize that he has had plans like this for us for weeks? Not that he was going to take any open action himself, of course. Too much danger in that. We silly youths could take all the chances and bear the brunt of the royal anger. But he will have the advantage of alliance with the royal house. He'll glory in it! He'll huff and he'll puff but he'll glory in it! The big disappointment to him is that you will not one day be king, if you are right about that. That his grandson will not be king."

Aurelius was shocked. What a ninny he was. The old count had been solicitous about him, careful not to notice how often his daughter rode out, and for how long, with the young stranger. Then he was relieved. At least no rages, no violent opposition to what had occurred this afternoon from one quarter anyway. Then he was amused at his own innocence. The king was right. The blood royal guaranteed that everyone would try to use you. Finally he was worried.

"What of you, Jimena? Will you be disappointed too that our son will never become the king?"

Jimena understood immediately the unspoken import of his question.

"Oh, Oro, Oro! Do you think that I would have brought Ram here? Or Neppy? No matter what my father wanted? I have come to be your wife because you won me. You yourself. I love you! That is all. Well—not quite. Of course, I like the idea that I have married a prince. What woman would not? Of course, I would like to see my son king someday. But I can be very much content with you—just dear, sweet, loving you. If your uncle is furious and decrees a new exile for you, I will go with you singing. Do you hear—singing!"

This last came from the girl with a rude force. She seized him and pressed her body closely to him. He answered with his own and for a moment they were both silent.

"I worry only that I may have married a man who is destined to become a monk. Do you have to go back to see your precious Alvitus again, Oro? My father would send someone to tell him that you are not returning and to collect your belongings."

"How could I do that, Jimena? He took me in—sheltered me. I do not want to go because he will storm at me. He will assure me that I am an utter fool. And I will feel like one. There is no chance that he will understand what you mean to me. Still, I must go. I owe him that courtesy."

"But I worry about his influence on you more than about the anger of the king, your uncle. You will stand up boldly to the king for you are no coward. But the old man has a power. What you tell me and how you regard him tells me that. And there is so much goodness in you that you will find it difficult to resist him just because you are so good and generous."

Jimena was pleading now. She was badly frightened and close to tears.

"Is he better than you?We have become one, you and I, now. Could I leave you? Ever? I swear that I shall return tomorrow. I swear that we shall never be parted by anyone. Can you not believe that?"

"I believe that you believe that. I am not so sure what the world and others can do to us. Give me a token. Give me yourself once more as a pledge. Then you can go."

And so the two embraced and made love yet once again that afternoon. Despite all their ardor there was also a certain desperation to it. The foreboding of his beloved had sounded an echo of doubt and apprehension in the mind of Aurelius that he could not entirely quell. Afterwards they went hand in hand but quietly back towards the palace of her father.

# Chapter Sixteen

Before long it would rain. The moon was full and well up but in the western sky dark thunderheads were boiling towards it. Still, Aurelius was loath to simply abandon the rabbit roasting on the stick. Jimena had given the cleaned carcass to him just before he had left her that evening. He was happy and ravenous and the juices of the coney were beginning to boil within it.

In a little while he was going to have to seek shelter from the storm that was brewing but for the present he wanted some time to recall the rich emotions experienced that marvelous day and to replenish some of the energies that he had spent. It was not a time to snack on the scraps and leavings that were the ordinary fare that Alvitus had to offer. Jimena had anticipated that that would be true and had provided for his need in advance. He smiled at the thought. It was warming.

He had brought the rabbit out here by the stream to prepare because it would have been embarrassing to eat in front of the old man. Not only was he implicitly rejecting what the hermit would have provided, as he had provided for so many weeks now, but Alvitus did not eat flesh meat on principle and neither had Oro while he resided with him. So he had moved with the carcass, his flint and steel, and a handful of shavings here. The early summer had been so dry that kindling was easy and it was only necessary to fashion a rough spit.

Aurelius moved, dreamlike in the afterglow of remembrance, though some part of his mind was aware that he should already be eating. Thunder was muttering out there and brief glows lit the interiors and the outer edges of the massing clouds. The bulk of them had now overtopped the moon and the night had become darker abruptly. His tiny fire lit no more than the few feet immediately surrounding him. The breeze that had sprung up some few minutes ago felt heavy from the ocean damp with which it was laden.

When he had told Alvitus of his decision to leave the old man had said nothing at all. He had remained absolutely silent while the young man had tried, with growing difficulty in the absence of any response, to explain his feelings to the man who had been his companion and spiritual guide for almost two months past. He had, of course, stressed his own conviction that he had no call such as his master had. He had dwelt on his experiences of his own inadequacy for contemplation and interior exploration despite his honest attempts to persevere. He brought in, grasping at the suggestion of an alternative duty, Count Muño's final recognition of himself as a member of the royal family and the need to attend on the impending visit of the king himself. At last and lamely, he had admitted to the hermit that he had fallen in love with the count's daughter. Of course he made no allusion to the particular events of the afternoon. But Oro did go so far as to confess their intention to marry and even asked for the approval of his friend.

Still there had been absolutely no response. The old man might as well have been mute. He might as well have been deaf. Not even a twitch. Not a frown. Oro had virtually fled before that hostile, unyielding withdrawal. He had taken his rabbit and his flint and had come out here with the idea that it would be easier, simpler, to sleep away under the stars. In the morning maybe he could try again. In any event, in the morning he was leaving. But now it looked as though he would have to go back to sleep in the old hut. It was going to be a bad night in more ways than one.

The staff caromed off his skull! Some premonition had moved him, at the last minute, and he had ducked and had taken less than its full force. Otherwise it would have left him unconscious in the midst of his own fire. As it was, sparks flew, burst, and died within the walls of his head. Only the pain of the embers as they ate through his tunic called his whirling mind back. He rolled to one side hastily, knocking over the spit. Hot greases from the coney baptized him anew and he continued to roll beyond the little blaze, scattering sticks and coals in every direction.

The staff pursued him yet. It bounced impartially off his back and off the ground when his flight from the fire eluded its swings.

"You young pig!" It was Alvitus. "The dog that returns to its own vomit! You dare to come back here with the stink of a woman full upon you. You take your greasy little fleshmeat carcass and build a fire upwind of me! Must I smell you and your bloody animal too? Have a broken bone or two for your penance!"

Oro rolled and fended off the staff when he could with his arms. He grabbed at the punishing implement but the dark and the surprising agility of the hermit frustrated his attempts. He had no desire to strike back, even if he could have made out the slight figure's whereabouts, and thus far the sudden attack had deprived him of wit and breath to shout for a halt.

The ground roared before it opened. The noise was a grinding of stone upon stone—like that of the hillside when it rushes down upon the land below in the aftermath of an extended rainy season. Except that it went on and on. The landslide ends in a minute and leaves devastation but also the profoundest silence in its wake.

As the ground roared it heaved. Aurelius continued to roll upon the ground but now his gyrations were not of his own making. He was rattled about like dice in the cup, from this side to that. His tormentor, caught with staff upraised to strike yet again, was pitched violently headlong upon the very body of his target. All else forgotten, the two now clung to one another while the maddened earth rocked them back and forth and shook them like terriers will a rat. So anxious was the ground to be rid of them that it actually heaved them up free from its surface only to have them fall back heavily with their combined weight. Neither could catch a breath but neither would have loosed his grip on the other. The utter blackness left them bereft of all reference and direction save that provided by the body of the other. By turns the weight of the one pummeled the other as their positions changed with the quaking of the world.

Even when the light came they were unable to see. For it came in rapid bolts that danced and dazzled, flared and died. Where it touched down the earth cried out in pain and writhed the more and threw up great rocks and trees against its torturer. The shafts of light then became more frequent, jostled and crowded, and overtook one another so that the glare of hell was rendered almost constant. Through squinted eyes almost drowning in their own juices, they could dimly catch the images. There, across the river in the forest, the massive pillars struck like burning spears. Without pause, almost at once, they tore and plunged among the trees of the forest. Where they met the ground great boles were flung into the air, sideways, end over end. And scarcely had their flares begun to dim when a dozen fires sprung up behind their progress. A corridor of flame began its procession in their wake—waving, dancing, leaping.

The very air itself was burnt and seared by the passage of the bolts. They choked on it and gasped for better, for it tasted of sulphur and bitter herbs. But great clouds of smoke began now to roll across the stream. The ashes and heat of the forest in flame descended upon them and they scrabbled for the stream's edge to soak their rags and to conceal their bodies beneath its coverlet. The surface of the stream mirrored and doubled the dancing inferno marching to its banks.

Like all else in this witch's cauldron the howling began somewhere towards the west. A thousand wolves in full throat, it rushed down upon them. Slammed into them and was gone! Overwhelmed by that screech, in the very next moment they could hear nothing for the wall of water that had trailed its march, fell in wave-like sequence, massive and unyielding, pressing them down, down below the surface of the river. They struggled for air. The violence of the downpour left them confused. The surface of the stream met and mingled with it.

The current came stronger against their bodies. The dryness of the spring had left a thousand baked rivulets and these, now filled to the brim with rushing water, poured their contents without let into the river itself. They could feel it pressing their being with new strength, redoubled urgency. Slipping and clawing they came to the bank and drew themselves out into a world hardly less wet. Exhausted, they crawled away from the clutching stream, the swelling stream. The darkness was stygian. To distinguish sound above the pounding of the torrential rain was impossible. Without words, driven by a common instinct, they sought alike to crawl towards what they hoped was higher ground.

Sight was useless. To stand erect, if their confusion and exhaustion had permitted it, would have only served to disorient them further. The mother surface of the land alone offered guidance. Along it they progressed like snails, seeking always the feeling of ascent. Finally, they ceased to move. Inert, they lay side by side under the unrelenting pummeling of the waters of the sky. Helpless, cold, they huddled together on the ground. Only where they touched was there warmth. At last, consciousness drained from them and they fainted.

*   *   *

As always, the sun rose. Its rays found reflection in a thousand tiny pools and a million droplets still suspended from the ends of leaves and branches. Its growing heat danced above the earth and extracted from it tendrils of mist, of steam, so that the earth itself became liquid, indistinct in the morning light. Insects trilled and buzzed and droned with the rich new life. Birds swooped and circled and complained about the remains of nest and egg amidst the woody debris scattered everywhere. Rabbits sat and shivered, awaiting the drain of water that would return their burrows. In the heights of the sky the hawks regarded their condition with growing interest.

The two men stirred. At first it was impossible to separate the return of consciousness from the shivering reflexes which had busied their bodies for the length of the night. But under the muddy rags, the body began to steam and so to redefine itself against the stinking cloth which held it captive. Aurelius could see his companion but for long was unable to bring himself to speak. The world about him was so new and so clean that he forbore to break in upon it. The man beside him shook suddenly and violently.

"You are alive, Alvitus?"

"We have come through it, Aurelius, we have come through it!"

"Yes, but our hut is gone. So are our clothes and supplies. My weapons too. The river has carried off everything we had. We're alive but whatever we had is gone. And we are both still as wet as watersnakes."

"Of course! We are reborn! The world has been reborn, Oro! Can't you feel it? The Lord has visited his people and nothing shall be the same!"

The old man was on his feet. His pathetic rags clung to his skinny body but he was suddenly as active as a boy.

"Come on, Aurelius."

Alvitus started off at a rapid pace towards the river. Oro watched him go, then rose more slowly and began to trail after the hermit.

"Are you coming?"

"Where are you going?"

"Where it is! Across the river! Where it all happened!"

Aurelius started with dismay. Had the storm—whatever it was—shaken the old man's mind loose?

"The river will be too high. We won't be able to cross it yet. We should wait until more of the runoff passes."

"Of course, we can cross. That is what He wants us to do. The Lord has pointed the way and we have been called to publish his glory."

Alvitus had come to the bank and stepped out boldly into the current where the ford had been. Farther and farther in he waded until the waters rose to his chest. But somehow the holy man continued to advance and the water actually began to drop away, first to his waist, then to his loins. His knees were just emerging!

Oro entered the stream himself. The old man was motioning impatiently. God it was cold. He had just begun to regain his body heat from the soaked rags that clung to him. Now he lost it entirely once more. By the time he reached the opposite shore he was again shivering uncontrollably.

"Hurry up, boy! Hurry up!"

And his companion set off at a jog into the nearest copse. Uncertainly, Oro began to hurry, then to trot in his wake. The man was like a squirrel. In every direction there were uprooted trees and great limbs severed from their trunks. Tangles of roots lay bare and sweating everywhere. Leaves and pine needles, branches without end blocked the view for minutes at a time. But Alvitus was nimble, agile, a man restored to his youth. He bounded forward and Oro followed grumbling and struggling. His own sweat was beginning to mingle unpleasantly with the moisture still trapped in his garments from the night before.

"Here, Aurelius, here!"

Beyond one more fallen branch he found himself in a space the size of a small farm where the forest cover had been completely leveled. Not a clearing really, for debris spread wherever he looked. In the midst of it Alvitus knelt, his hands and head raised to the heavens. Oro could scarcely glimpse him above the refuse of vegetation that littered the ground.

"Kneel, Aurelius, kneel! You have found yourself on holy ground! This is the day the Lord has made! Rejoice and be glad!"

Oro knelt. His friend felt something, surely. Or he saw something. But what. He looked about him and all was desolation and destruction. The aftermath of the storm. The most terrifying storm that he had ever known. What was it that his friend had found?

Roving, his eye caught a fragment of color on the ground as a random ray of sunlight glanced from it. Reaching down he retrieved what appeared to be a small rock, about the size of his hand, with a colored surface, a flat surface on one side. As he peeled the wet, spongy clay from it he found himself looking at a leaf. It was a leaf worked in tiny stones of green, and gray, and yellow. Exploring the edges with his fingers, he discovered that the colored stones were attached to a fragment of cement. It was a piece of mosaic. Somewhere here there had once been a decorated wall or a floor. Roots from a falling tree had torn it up with them!

Alvitus still knelt. He seemed to be in a trance. His attitude was that of prayer but no words came from his mouth. His lips were still. He was oblivious to Oro's presence.

The young man stood again while his companion remained unaware of his movement. Concentrating now, Oro looked about closely. Gradually, one after the other, regular forms began to reveal themselves amidst the piles of sylvan refuse. Here a worked stone, its exposed side washed by the torrents of rain of the evening before and now beginning to glint in the sunshine. There, a corner. A right angle of granite almost buried beneath the crown of a fallen tree. Both something that men alone made. And at the base, where the angle of stone enclosed its space, more color. There once had been a flooring of mosaic here in this copse.

Just ahead the hermit had raised himself with a jerk from his devotions. He looked about where he stood, shook his head impatiently, and then started back towards Oro.

"We've got to get some help here. This whole place must be cleared. It would take you and me too long to do it. We'll get the villagers to help. Come along. Come along."

He's like a cat. After that beating last night how can he be so nimble? He should be dead. We both should be.

More gingerly than the old man, Aurelius followed, wondering. He was, however, close enough to see the result when Alvitus emerged from the woods at the edge of the stream. On the far bank a large number of the villagers had gathered. Now they involuntarily fell back some steps as they saw him. The young man realized that the country people at first were not sure that this was not a spirit rather than a man. Then, when he himself stepped clear of the trees their reaction was much the same. Probably they had come down to see what was left to be buried.

"You there! You there, Miro! Wait right there!"

And the old man plunged anew into the waters at the ford. After a brief hesitation, Oro did the same. This day is going to be largely spent, he thought, before I am dry. By the time he reached the far shore Alvitus was already locked in argument with the village headman.

"We thought that you were dead, for sure, old man. We came down to scrape your bones together and plant them in the ground."

"You are as much a fool as ever, Miro. Why would I be dead? The Lord brought me here. Why would he kill me? He has work for me yet. Did you have many killed in the village?"

"We didn't have any. The storm never touched us. It only hit down here. But we could see it clear enough."

The headman shifted uneasily on his crutch. He could see how strongly his words affected these two. Their reaction gave point and form to his own feelings about the peculiar nature of last night's storm. They had thought that the whole district had been hit. But everywhere else had been spared.

Abruptly, Alvitus found his tongue. "Well, then you have all your plow teams still. We'll need all three of them. Bring the oxen and their traces, some tackle, but leave off the plows. And get as many axes and billhooks as you have. There's a lot of ground to be cleared before dark."

"Wait a moment, old man. Ground cleared where? For who?"

"For the Lord God, that's who, you great pagan! And over there across the stream in the forest. By the ruins."

The men gathered around Miro muttered and shifted from foot to foot. Their leader himself paled and looked from Oro to Alvitus uneasily.

"I don't think that we'll get anyone to go in there. It's bad luck, that grove. Especially after last night. Leave it well enough alone. Leave it to the spirits."

"You are a great ignorant oaf, Miro. It is not evil spirits that call to you from that copse. It is the Lord of Hosts. Your God wants you. Not only you but the whole world will be going in there before long and the Lord has chosen you and your people to be the first. Get the oxen, man!"

Miro and the village men began to edge away. In a moment they would be in headlong flight. Their former shepherd had always been a queer one and perhaps even a warlock. They would not have been surprised to see him disappear in a cloud of smoke even now. By any reckoning he should be dead. Now he spoke like one possessed.

"Do you know who I am, headman?"

Aurelius had been silent up until now but he intervened because he could see the desire of the villagers for escape. His words pulled Miro up short. The man had heard the news. The whole valley had heard it within a day of the return of the count's men from Oviedo.

"Yes, my lord. We have been told that you are cousin to the great king who is in Oviedo."

"And to the great king who will be here shortly. The king who will be greatly desirous of seeing the wonder there across the river. You will get much credit, all of you, for having made it possible for him to view it. I think that you will be well rewarded for your labors. Now go and get the ox teams and bring them down here as Alvitus has asked."

He watched their faces closely as he spoke. They were still uneasy at the prospect of what they were to do but there were traces of cupidity as well—and curiosity at this talk of kings. They stirred, and looked at one another. Miro decided that he would take the lead before this puppy took it from him.

"All right! Get the teams! And the rest of the stuff. You heard the young lord."

Bowing awkwardly on his single leg, he began to herd his fellows back up the hill. The hermit looked after them with exasperation and some contempt.

"Bloody barbarians! They'll do more for their king than they will for their God. Well, wait till they see what's over yonder. Then we'll see who has the power."

With this he glanced at Oro as if to challenge him. The experience that the two companions had suffered the night before could never be undone. Still, both understood as well that their paths had diverged. Alvitus had watched this morning when his dream had been realized, his vision confirmed. Sorrowfully, he had seen that Aurelius had not been granted the understanding of it. The boy was outside. If he had really been sent, it was for some other purpose.

But his own joy, coupled with his impatience, gave him no time to dwell on it.

Aurelius, for his part, was awed and confused by what had happened. Clearly Alvitus knew that his long vigil was over. The fundamental thing had been accomplished. The young man felt again the power of belief that radiated from the old man. Yet Oro had no idea what it was that had changed, that had come to pass. He had interfered to enlist the help of the villagers, had spoken solemnly in his uncle's name, and he had no real understanding of what it was that had been revealed nor what its import would be.

# Chapter Seventeen

The work was well advanced by the time that the bishop and the count and their party arrived at the scene. At first there had been a problem getting the oxen to ford the stream. The usually stolid beasts apparently sensed something of the apprehension of their masters, the villagers. True to their nature, they did nothing violent. They simply balked at the least opportunity, on the bank of the river, in midstream, on the far side. Then, when the accumulation of abuse finally moved them, there was the difficulty of threading the bulky animals through the thickets of downed vegetation that now constituted the nearest stretch of forest. When finally hitched in teams for the actual hauling the animals seemed more at ease in that familiar situation.

The task had been nightmarish to begin with. The debris was so extensive that the first question arose over where to put it. Any location chosen soon proved a new obstacle to the clearing. After several false starts Aurelius discovered a small path at the far edge of the devastation and set some of the men to widening it with axes and billhooks. Then, after they had made some progress, it could be used as a road along the sides of which the ox teams could deposit their loads farther from the principal scene of the work.

Nevertheless, before any one could begin to see that their collective labors were having an effect, the day had advanced well past noon. The heat had become intense, for the surrounding forest blocked what minor breeze the summer day offered. Moreover, the pervasive dampness from the drenching rains of the previous night enveloped the workers, drenched their clothes, and made every surface slick and potentially dangerous.

Some of the village women had appeared with provisions and a lot of the men had quit to eat. The women at the site, who had been working during the morning to clear the lighter rubbish to an area where it might subsequently be burned, paused in their work to exchange complaints and observations with the newcomers. Worse, most of the village toddlers had arrived with their mothers and now wandered about jumping on this and that, trying to ride the oxen, playing and fighting, and generally putting themselves in danger of being crushed each time a heavy load was set in motion.

Aurelius had assumed direction of the work largely because his was the only authority on the scene equal to that role. As a member of the royal household, his status was so exalted here that all other vanished by the mere fact of his presence. Alvitus, in his new dignity as wonderworker and prophet, might have been able to prevail ultimately but the old man was everywhere at once and, consequently, nowhere when he might have been useful. The greater the area cleared, the more agitated he became. He issued orders faster than the men could possibly work and surely faster than they were willing to work. One command piled on top of another until ox drivers looked helplessly at Oro to resolve the contradictions. More than once he had, gently but physically, to draw his old friend out of the way when the latter dashed in to examine a newly revealed object or bit of architecture.

So it had gone for five or six hours now. The young man

could see that enough had been done to make clear the perimeter of an old building, the foundations, parts of two columns, but only odds and ends of walls, collapsed and broken. Here and there, where roots had pushed up or where the drag of heavy loads had deeply scored the surface, were the emerging traces of what seemed to be an extensive mosaic pavement. But he hadn't yet a really good idea of the extent or nature of what they had found and most of the workmen from the village had even less. They were too close to the work to really see it.

Increasingly, they had found some reason or pretext to halt work now. Their former superstitious dread of the ruins seeped back as they had time to recall it. The idleness was contagious and Oro was unsure that he could reverse the tendency. He decided that he must somehow enlist the aid of Miro. The one-legged headman had spent most of the time sulking. It was not the sort of work that his condition allowed him to do. Under other circumstances, that is in Aurelius' absence, he would have directed it. But his own neighbors looked rather to the young man and so Miro harassed the women for want of better occupation. When the former approached him, the headman ignored him for as long as he could pretend not to notice.

Then, before the argument had a chance to develop, someone shouted, "The count! The count has come himself."

Aurelius turned in the direction of the river in time to see Count Muño, Bishop Teodemiro, together with the bailiff and a score of warriors, enter the growing clearing by way of the new path from the river. His heart leaped to see that Jimena was also with the party. When he turned back he could see that, remarkably, just about everyone among the villagers was hastening back to work. Apparently they took the arrival of the count on the scene as a sign of his interest, of his approval, and none of them had the least doubt about the wisdom of furthering the count's interests energetically. Ironically, Oro was much less sure of the count's reaction to the enterprise.

Alvitus! In the name of God, where was the man? Count Muño and Bishop Teodemiro are approaching and the one person who will have to explain what is happening and why is off prying under some branches or scraping at some dirt. Jimena is smiling at me anxiously and I can't ignore her but I need to find the old man. Jesus!

"Miro. Find Alvitus and bring him here. Right now!"

The headman stared at him, not yet really accustomed to the fact of his authority, and then, remembering it with a start, mumbled assent and hobbled off. Aurelius turned his attention to the count. He could hardly greet the man's daughter before the man himself. Or before the bishop.

"You are welcome, excellencies. I would have sent someone across the river to guide you if I had known of your approach."

He smiled as sincerely as he could. Miro, he supposed, had sent off some messenger to the count even before they had begun work. Of course, he had not mentioned it to Alvitus or to Aurelius. The latter would have wanted to get some idea of what the work would yield before informing the count but the bacon was already in the fire.

He turned to Jimena who was searching his face closely.

"And it is very good to see you again, my Lady Jimena."

With that he took her hand and pressed it briefly but firmly to his lips. The young woman colored slightly and her eyes glistened. She smiled with a relief and a contentment that was only too evident. He knew that she too had heard the tale of the night just past and had feared, probably, for both his safety and for his continued dedication to her.

Glancing sidelong at the the count and his brother, Oro knew as well that his beloved had not informed them of what had passed between the two of them. Surely the count could guess now but the time for a formal approach was still to come. It pleased the young man that he had nonetheless taken the initiative in declaring their future.

"Have your excellencies had word of what passed here last night? Do you know of the strange and terrible storm that visited the district?"

"We have had word of very little else this morning. But suppose that you tell us too, my Lord Aurelius. How did you come through the night?"

The count's visage reflected as much as he dared of his impatience and displeasure with what he heard and with what he saw before him. This puppy has taken a lot into his hands all of a sudden. I asked him to keep things as quiet as possible and now he has put an entire village of mine to work on God knows what. Worse, from the look of that smirk on my daughter's face, he's been tampering with more than the loyalty of my villagers. If he wanted to complicate my life with my brother and with my enemies he could hardly have done better.

"I came through the night, my good count, on my stomach like a crab in the mud. I had my face in the ground, and my arms over my head, and prayers on my lips. Even then I think I would not have lasted much longer if it had not stopped when it did. Your own eyes can see the destruction around you and begin to guess at what a storm it was."

Indeed, the count and his brother already had been taken back by what they had seen. Neither one of them could recall destruction on this scale that was yet so concentrated.

Outside of this little district, no one in the region had experienced the storm, not even in the small village immediately adjoining it.

"A strange storm for sure." It was Bishop Teodemiro. "But perhaps no stranger than what is going on here now. What is happening here, my Lord Aurelius? You have an entire village at work in the midst of a forest. It hardly seems like an occupation for good, Christian folk."

"I really wish that I could tell you that, my good bishop. I am not sure that I know. It is only that Alvitus believes that the storm was a sign from heaven that the forest should be opened here. I think that he expects something to be revealed. As soon as Miro finds him, the holy man can tell you in his own words."

Jimena groaned inside but kept her peace. Will he ever learn not to tell the truth to his enemies? He has obviously taken charge here and so he is responsible. Now he admits in front of my father and his brother that he is not sure why! I love him for his honesty and goodness. But these two don't!

"A sign from heaven?" This came from the bishop. "Are we diviners of spirits here? I had heard that some such words were used, carelessly, in front of this rabble. They are dangerous words. And you have seen fit to put actions to them, my lord. An older man, a wiser, calmer man, like the king himself, might have chosen to act less hastily. Now we are going to have to devise a remedy for this unfortunate hysteria."

"A remedy! A remedy for the work of God! Is that how you discharge your calling, bishop?"

It was Alvitus, who had chosen his own time to appear and his own combative manner to intervene. Oro could tell by the harsh set of his mentor's face and the tone of his mouth that he had come prepared, rather seeking, a conflict.

The hermit had come slowly, deliberately, leaving him to flounder in the first acts of the confrontation. He courts death. He's a soldier on campaign and he fully intends to win. I should leave him to his martyrdom! At this moment, Oro felt the bishop and the count to be more congenial. But geniality is not one of my teacher's virtues, he thought.

"The work of God? The work, of God, old man? I decide what the works of God are. Not some ignorant, ex-shepherd who has no sacrament, no unction, and no authority."

"Will you decide against the will of the Divine Himself, bishop? If He calls me instead of you, that burns in your gut doesn't it? Like the Pharisees of old. You reject the work because you are too blind to see it, to recognize it under your own nose."

Hermit and bishop were shouting at one another now. Some of the village people had stopped work to listen and to enjoy the fight. Count Muño knew that he could not let this brawl continue. His authority was involved here too. Older warriors in his following recognized the signs of the count's uneasiness. There will be some blood here. Swords were loosened. The count moved closer to the hermit.

"So far, old man, who has seen signs? You? We have seen the effects of a storm. A severe storm and a funny one perhaps. Strangely concentrated, maybe, but such things happen. Only you read it as a work of the Lord. And, as my brother says, no one has made the work of the Lord the province of an old soldier, a derelict sheepherder! You look above your station, man. You stake a claim to power not given to you. People die for that, as you know. You've killed a few yourself in the olden days."

Oro feared for his friend just now. Killing was in the air and Alvitus had put himself in jeopardy with his own mouth. The young man was not sure that he could save him. He would try but his uncle himself would not likely support a ragged country fellow who claimed to be the prophet of the Lord against one of his own bishops. Even kings usually respected the peculiar jurisdiction of the high clergy. Alvitus, however, seemed heedless of his peril.

"Your affection for your brother, noble count, clouds your own vision as well. Who has seen a storm such as this? Has my pupil, Aurelius, described it to you? Did he tell you of the shaking and the groaning of the earth? Did he tell of the lightning, falling swifter, more frequent than the arrows of the Africans, tearing and setting the land afire? Did you hear from him of a deluge so strong and so thick that a frog could have swum in it if the frogs themselves had not been drowned? Yes, I saw all this, as he did, and I know it to have been the work of our God. I declare it to have been so! Do you dare to contradict me, count?"

So this is what Oro saw, Jimena thought. This man, he has a power and he dares to use it. This struggle can end in only one fashion, but Oro's Alvitus will beard them all. I was right to worry about Oro leaving me to follow him.

Bishop Teodemiro looked impatiently at his brother. How much provocation would Muño allow before he acted? The noble turned as if to speak to his guard.

"I should let you set them on me. I should let you loose your thugs." It was Alvitus again. "Then you would feel the retaliation of the Lord towards those who interfere with His servants. You would fall like Herod and your very bowels burst from your skin and the dogs would eat your entrails!

"But I will have mercy, count, on you and your unbelieving brother both. I will show you a sign that will convince even the obstinate. Follow me."

The old man turned and abruptly set off towards the center of the clearing. Bishop and count looked uncertainly at one another and then hastened after him, the latter signaling his guard to follow. Oro and Jimena fell in behind them. When the party halted it was before a small rectangular depression in the center, or so it seemed, of what remained of the mosaic pavement. A couple of villagers were just about finished scraping from it a mixture of dirt, small twigs, and decayed leaves. As they did another mosaic pattern emerged, this one intact. Central in it was a conch shell.

"You see! You see!" Alvitus was almost dancing with excitement. "I have loved O Lord the beauty of your house and the place where your glory dwells. Break it open! Break it open!" This to the workmen. And after glancing for permission at the count who nodded just perceptibly, one of them began to swing a heavy hammer against the paving.

"The sign that you have for us then is an old Roman grave?" Bishop Teodemiro felt the need to reassert his control over events. "Old bones mouldering these centuries and better left undesecrated by a profane, half-demented old shepherd."

"Yes, that is the sign, bishop. Old bones. Old bones that the Lord wished the world to know again. Old bones that the Lord called me here to discover. Old bones whose reemergence to the light he has compelled even stiff-necks like you, like your brother and his noble warriors, to come and witness. So that in future ages no one will be able to say that only a crazy old man and a youth scarcely attained to manhood invented them."

The bishop was not quite sure now that he any longer had the advantage here. The audacity of the hermit was unsettling. Nevertheless, he had to continue. He could hardly retreat before all of these people, his own brother, the king's cousin.

"What bones then? Whose bones do you suppose that you have found. What would you have us believe?"

This last exchange had fallen into a growing silence and a spreading uneasiness. Everyone present was listening. Intent.

"I tell you what the Lord has revealed to me. These are the bones of the Apostle James, the brother of the Lord!"

There was a quick intake of breath on the part of many. Others stepped back a few paces, not sure now that they should have come at all. Count Muño thought grimly that sometimes it was good to have a brother who had to deal with this sort of thing.

"Hold your tongue, man! The Apostle James? Do you know the penalty for blasphemy? James was bishop in Jerusalem. He was executed, beheaded, there by order of the tyrant, Herod. His head was put on a spike and his body was thrown on a dungheap outside the holy city."

"His body is here, bishop! It has been buried here ever since. It is buried here because he preached here. James founded the Christian church in Hispania."

"I have heard it said so, that the Apostle James preached in this peninsula. But I have never heard anyone dare to assert that he was buried here. Not unless they were heretics of the stripe of Priscillian and his hangers-on. Is that what you are? Is that where you have heard this nonsense? You have erred in meddling with a learning that is beyond your talents, warlock!"

"I have never heard of your Priscillian. I know that the bones of Saint James are buried under this ground where you stand because the Lord has revealed it to me. No more, no less!"

At this last, Bishop Teodemiro recovered his composure.

"And isn't it curious that when the Lord speaks to the

ignorant and the lowly that the message is always so strange, so peculiar? It is fortunate, one thinks, that he has appointed his bishops to guard the true faith. The faith would soon become very odd indeed if every ragged prophet were to have their way with it. We are supposed to believe that the bones of the Apostle James rest here beneath us because God told you it is so. Is that it, old man?"

Alvitus' eyes flashed and he drew himself up to his full height. There was about him the most extraordinary self-possession. Slowly he surveyed those assembled there. Then a sardonic smile spread across his visage. He spoke hardly more than a whisper.

"No, just because the Lord revealed this to me, you do not have to accept it, my lord bishop. He is about to give you a sign all of your own. Then you yourself will give testimony to the truth of what I have said—of what the Lord has revealed. Pray that you prove worthy of the revelation."

Ignoring the flabbergasted bishop, the hermit turned then to the workmen who were just clearing the debris of the mosaic and cement from the bottom of the depression.

"What do you see there?'

"Only a large rock, no more."

"Idiot, it is no rock. Lift it out! Lift it out!"

The men tried but it resisted their efforts. Their own legs were in the way and the thing was almost as large as the hole within which it sat. Finally, using a tree limb as a prise, they managed to slant one end of it up. Then, using two others behind it on the lower end, they raised it to the degree that they were able to get beneath it and heave it free.

Clear it came! A marble sarcophagus. It gleamed in the sunlight, fresh as the day on which it was fashioned despite its long sleep below the earth. The sides were richly worked. Closely seen, seaweed floated and fish glided amidst it. Sea horses hovered, sea urchins tumbled, and turtles swam effortlessly below the single ship that rode the surface. But the lid bore only a raised, single conch shell.

"Back! Back! Everyone get back! Make room for the lord bishop."

Alvitus' voice was hardly a necessary incitement. The marble casket seemed not merely to reflect the sun's rays. It appeared to gleam, to pulse with a light of its own. The little knot of people withdrew farther and farther from it in a mood of awe, an attitude approaching terror. Jimena and Oro, the Count Muño and Bishop Teodemiro were left standing clear before the coffin with the hermit. Though the legs of each felt as insubstantial as water, they were transfixed before it.

"Now excellency, remove the lid."

Alvitus thrust a chisel and a small mallet into Teodemiro's hands. There was a sound, an escape of collective breath, almost like a sigh from the assembled onlookers. Women gathered their children to them and men shifted anxiously from foot to foot.

The bishop was white to the lips. Unsteadily he moved towards the marble cask. Between the body of it and the lid he could see a line of lead, unbroken. Starting at the nearest corner, he positioned the chisel's blade against the sealer and struck it sharply. A piece flew free and he started back. There was a murmur form the crowd. The prelate was sweating profusely now but his sweat was cold. In a panic to finish he drove the chisel again and again around the course of the lid. When he reached the far side his features, taut with strain, were visible to all. Finally, it was done.

"Remove the lid, Bishop Teodemiro!"

The man looked at Alvitus, and then to the nearest workmen who stirred uneasily.

"No, no one else. Just you, just the bishop of the district. No one else can be involved in the witness. This is why you were called, man."

He was a large man, the bishop, still well-muscled though no longer young. He did not require physical help except that a peculiar tingling and prickling of his body left him awkward and clumsy. At the command of Alvitus, a tremor ran through him. None-the-less, he took one edge of the lid and slowly swung the whole of it sideways so that it was balanced across the coffin's foot.

"Look inside, excellency." The voice of Alvitus was merciless. "Look inside and tell us what it is you see."

Slowly, as the paralyzed crowd watched, the prelate's gaze moved over the casket's interior.

"What is it? What is it that you see? Make your witness, man! Declare the glory of the Lord!"

The insistence of the hermit was frightening in itself. Bishop Teodemiro was trembling violently. The farthest back in the crowd could see him quake. His throat twitched and his words came in a croak.

"Bones! The bones of the Apostle James!"

Triumphantly, Alvitus voice sang out once more.

"And how is it that you now know, lord bishop, that these are indeed the bones of the apostle of the Lord? What sign has the Lord given you?"

"There is no skull!"

# Chapter Eighteen

The palace of the count was entirely surrounded by the tents of the royal party. In fact, there was little open space at all left and the horses, mules, and oxen of the king's entourage overflowed the small corral of the count and pressed right up to the huts and gardens of the attendant village. There they milled, and jostled, and fouled the ground thoroughly despite the best efforts of the grooms to clear the excrement and the interest of the peasants themselves in collecting fertilizer for the next planting. More and more the stock was driven out daily over increasing distances for their number had quickly depleted such grazing as was available there and indeed had trampled the ground around into sodden muck.

The smell of animals mingled with the smell of men. While the king's party was small, numbering no more than two hundred, it more than doubled the usual inhabitants of the comital clearing and fields. Food was being collected for miles about to spare the dwindling stocks of the village. Water for people was not a problem, fortunately, for the local springs were ample but the livestock had to be watered at some distance whenever it was taken out to graze. New latrines had had to be dug almost immediately on the arrival of the royal troupe and everyone strictly admonished to use them exclusively. Still, fecal odors hung heavy on the moist summer air for large distances about them. The royal government functioned best when in regular motion. Any protracted stop tended to make it its own most dangerous foe.

Count Muño himself had taken up residence in one of the royal tents for King Alfonso had been weary of camp life by the time that he arrived from Oviedo and so had been installed in the comital palace. Bishop Teodemiro occupied another of the royal tents. The original plan to move everyone down to the coast at Iria Flavia had been abandoned as a consequence of the miraculous discovery of the relics of Santiago. The curiosity of the king about every detail connected with the event was near insatiable. He would not hear of proceeding on to the episcopal palace at the port. The king had himself walked about and inspected the site no fewer than four times since his arrival.

In the comital palace Alfonso utilized the count's private chamber rather than the great hall to conduct a personal inquest into the manner of the discovery of the remains of Saint James. Even his closest counselors were excluded for fear that the very nature of the questions which he put would disclose the character of his interest or the bent of his intentions. The king wanted as free a hand for his ultimate decision as the circumstances allowed. Naturally, despite all his warnings, the lesser folk interviewed would gossip and speculate furtively thereafter about the royal designs. But the emphasis on secrecy actively discouraged the bishop, the count, and the important nobles of the district from indulging in more of the same. The king could be arbitrary with even the greatest of his retainers and servitors. Safety lay above all in deference.

Alfonso was clad this morning in his habitual black, broken only by the splendor of a massive jeweled gold necklace that hung well down his chest. Even without the latter, the hint and concession to his past constituted by the rich black garments would not have deceived. Here was no monk. The dark, searching eyes, the poised concentration, the natural expectation of unquestioning obedience—all alerted the beholder to the true position of the man.

Jimena felt the dread that the royal presence inspired. He is a truly terrible man. Oro could have found no father here. No wonder that he and Ram and Neppy were so close. None of them could have sought affection from this wolf. And not even a queen to soften him—or to be soft in his stead.

"So then, young woman, you have no more information about the discovery of the body except for what others have told you? You were present the day it was exhumed, you saw the conditions of the forest thereabouts, you witness that the sarcophagus was sealed when it was taken from the ground, that the old man said in advance of its opening that it contained the body of the Apostle James, that no one but the bishop touched or opened the casket, and that he then immediately recognized what he found as those holy relics? Of events before that morning you have no direct, personal knowledge?"

"Just as you say, my lord king."

"Yet you are the daughter of a count. You surely heard your father and his brother, the bishop, talk about this Alvitus."

"Yes, lord. But they thought that he was crazy. They considered him a fanatic who might cause trouble but they hesitated to take action against him because of the effect it might have on the people of the district. Sooner or later they would have acted, I think."

"Sooner or later, every fool will act, young lady! Too late usually. But that character defect is not yours. I think that my nephew must have told you, above all people, something of this Alvitus."

"He did, sir. Aurelius was never sure until that day that the hermit was truly holy. He had his own doubts. He thought sometimes that the man could well be insane. But he never spoke of Alvitus except as a good man, a truly spiritual man, even if he might be dangerous. These things he said not only to me but to my father and to the bishop."

"So those two have told me themselves, even if not quite as impartially as have you."

There was a silence as the king regarded her. His nephew was lucky. She was well-favored. She also knew that she was a beautiful woman. The dark green of her tunic, the armlets of gold, the carefully worked and piled auburn tresses, her very carriage; all these testified to a mind that would make conscious use of her femininity to reach her ends. She had chosen that path even now with her king! And what was it that she wanted?

"Well, if you can tell me no more about the finding of the relics, let us then consider your own situation. Certainly it has not been marked by a failure to act. But how exactly do you describe your relationship to my nephew Aurelius?"

"We are lovers, my lord. I carry his child in my body."

"You cannot possibly be sure of that, young woman. You hope that it is so. You want to force the issue."

"I know it, your majesty. I know it. In another month you can have a woman you trust examine me and she will tell you that I am right."

The king regarded her with interest. She dared much. He tried another approach.

"Irony of ironies. I exile my nephew for an attempt at the rape of one maiden and I find him here guilty of the seduction of another."

The girl stiffened visibly and spoke with some heat.

"Oro did not attempt to rape that girl. It was a trap set by his enemies and yours, majesty. I believe that you now know that—but there is something more you should know. He did not seduce me. If anything, you might say that I seduced him. But he loves me. Ask him."

"The worse for you. Both you and my nephew knew, did you not, that he was not free to take a wife without my permission? The two of you have not dared to formalize a marriage but you are trying to force both myself and your father into permitting such an action. Why should I let myself be bullied by two striplings who have no idea of the political consequences of such a union? How have the two of you presumed to take such a step?"

"Because Oro loves me, majesty, and I love him. I chose to act in the fashion that I did because I feared to lose him—to you yourself or to Alvitus and his God. It is all the same. I would risk death rather than part with him."

"You do risk precisely that now. Do you understand that I can have you strangled?"

"Your majesty would have to have more than just I myself strangled. Oro himself, I think. Possibly my father."

"All of this could be done. If I should decide that the matter is important enough to justify it, it will be done."

"And what then will your majesty have left to rule? Is it that you wish to be served only by those that fear you? Is it for such a kingdom that you plan and struggle?"

The king was impressed and was pleased to be so defied. The young woman was no fool. She was obviously terrified. She was fighting not to tremble. He could read the signs of fear from long experience. Yet still she defied him!

"Do you think, child, that a kingdom is ruled without fear? The danger that Aurelius and you constitute is exactly that you may demonstrate that the king may be withstood—that his will may be set at naught. That is a dangerous example. What do I hope to gain that would compensate for such a risk?"

"Your permission, my lord and king, would gain you the most devoted of servants. Oro loves and admires you. He would have you as a father if it were possible. Such service is not for purchase but it needs to be rewarded. For myself, I would support your nephew—and yourself—in every way possible all the days of my life. Neither one of you will find a more faithful ally. Nor will you find a more constant friend, if I may presume to say it."

She would bargain with me! Alfonso was amused now as well as impressed. My nephew could be a very lucky man indeed. I wonder if he can learn to manage this woman?

"You plead your case well, young lady, though perhaps over boldly. However, I will talk more with Aurelius of this. Meanwhile, you will say nothing to anyone of the matter. On that I will not be disobeyed. When you leave, tell my nephew that I wish to see him. Tell him just that and no more."

The king made the briefest of dismissive signs with his right hand. Jimena puzzled over that severe countenance. For an instant she thought that she might have seen a hint of laughter in those eyes.

Aurelius entered in his turn, bowed slightly, and stood silently before the king. Jimena had been shaken when she emerged but she had told him nothing. Not knowing how or where to begin, he said nothing. The king too was silent for a little time. Finally, he began.

"What you have already told me about the circumstances of the finding of the relics of the Apostle has been borne out by the others whom I have questioned, Aurelius. But it appears that you alone really know this Alvitus. You lived with him for two months or so. That was a strange thing for a member of the royal house to do."

"I suppose that it was, sir. I had been ill. The ring that you had given me was stolen. I had no way to prove my identity here. Still, it is clear to me now that it would have been better to have gone directly to the count."

"So you don't wonder that the count suspected some conspiracy or other?"

"No, sir. It seems reasonable."

"And Alvitus, he took you in, fed you and lent you a roof, more or less. Was that because he believed in your royal lineage, do you suppose?"

"No, majesty, he had done that before he could possibly have known who I was. If anything he was disappointed to find that I was of your family. I think that he still is. He wanted me to be his disciple, his aide in the work to which he thought that he was called. Nothing else matters to him."

"Do you believe, Aurelius, that he has a call from God?"

"I do, sir. I did not for long, although I knew from the first that he was a most unusual, a strange sort of man. He is a hard, blunt man but honest. Now, it seems to me that the finding of the relics proves his call. Do you not think so?"

"If the relics are what they are, Aurelius. Have they worked a miracle yet?'

"Wouldn't you say, sir, that the storm itself was a miracle?"

"Perhaps I might if I had experienced it myself. Do you think that it was?"

"Yes, sir. I have never known anything like it. I believe that it has to have been God's work."

"Well, on that you agree with our good bishop and his brother, the count. And they are most reluctant witnesses, that is sure."

Alfonso was satisfied with the youth's demeanor so far. He gives a good account of himself. He accepts the blame for his acts and has not tried to trench on our relationship. No excuses. He is still as honest as he always has been.

"Well, let us say then, Aurelius, that we have here a saint, a holy man, who wants you for a disciple. Is that your calling as well?"

"No, your majesty. When I first came to this place I did try to follow in Alvitus' path. Since he fasted, I fasted. Since he prayed, I prayed. Since he meditated in silence, I meditated in silence. But I don't think that I have a vocation. Nothing seemed to work for me as it did for him."

"Or it may be that you found a more attractive calling? I must say, that is a beautiful woman."

Oro colored. The sudden change of direction caught him off guard even though he had known that it must come at some point. His confusion was evident.

"I don't know what to say to that, sir. It must seem so. I have wondered about it myself for some little time. I had never been in love before. Finally, I decided that what I most wanted was to be with her. Whether that means that I have betrayed my true call or that I have found it, I am not entirely sure. But I have made my decision."

To his own surprise, Alfonso found himself choked momentarily by the sincerity of the young man. This boy would have made a son! This is the dream that I surrendered a long time ago. But he forced himself to continue in the same tenor.

"You seem to have made a wide variety of decisions. I have been told that you actually chose to protect this hermit against my own count and my own bishop. I am further informed that you commandeered an entire village of the count's to get the forest about the tomb cleared. Just this morning I have learned that you took it on yourself to become betrothed without either my permission or that of the count and that you have gotten his daughter with child."

Jimena didn't tell me! She can't be sure! Or is she still afraid that I will desert her? What do I say to protect her best. To protect them both!

"Your majesty, in most matters I have acted in the way in which I might best serve your interests. I was in exile and had no way to consult with you or to defer to you. But it did not seem to me that to allow the bishop or the count to persecute the holy man was wise. Once the storm had testified to a presence, it also seemed to me that we could do no other thing than to discover the real meaning of that witness quickly.

"You will judge, of course, as to whether I was right. But it may be that in this other matter as well, I will have served you properly. It could be that your majesty will soon have a grand-nephew of your lineage."

The impertinence of the youth! But the king made at least one of the decisions facing him. Allowing a smile for the first time, he replied to the boy.

"You do seem to have the most marvelous luck, Oro. While I am not yet positive, it does begin to seem to me that your instincts have been altogether sound. God knows, I do approve of your choice of that young woman. Yet it surprises me that you have so quickly developed the ability to act. That pleases me if it does not altogether excuse you.

"Now you know that I have sent Ramiro south with the army this spring. That means that I believe that he will succeed me as king. Does that disappoint you or your betrothed?"

"No, uncle. I suspected that you would do so anyway and

I have already told Jimena that you would. We both accept that with all good will."

"You should understand Oro that I did so because I think that Ramiro has a hardness about him that you lack. Kings must be hard—often cruel. I am not sure that you could be so. You have shown that you can be strong, even brave, but these are not quite the same thing.

"You also know that I have set Nepotian to study. He is very bright but he lacks the sort of dogged integrity that you and Ramiro share. He might make an excellent counselor but he sees, I think, a few too many possibilities in any situation to be safe commanding men. What do you think of that decision."

"I think that you have the wisdom that graces a king, uncle."

Alfonso stared at the young man. This is not the time or place for me to laugh aloud, surely. In good humor and with open affection now, he dismissed him.

"And you are developing the manners of a churchman, Oro. When you leave, seek out that young woman and tell her that she and you have my blessing. But before you do, have my guard bring in your friend Alvitus."

When the hermit was led in, accompanied by two sturdy men-at-arms, he proved to be bound and hobbled. Alfonso directed that he be freed and then sent the warriors away.

"So you are the author of all this disturbance," he began.

"No, I am not, sire. God is the 'author of all this disturbance' as you choose to put it."

"So you say. So you say. Speak right out, old man, as one former soldier to another. Are you then a 'holy man'?"

"People have called me that, your majesty. But I've cut my share of throats—just as you have. I regret all of that now but I must say that I don't feel like a different man. I'm the same old Alvitus."

"Well supposing that God wanted to reveal the tomb of one of his apostles, why should he pick 'the same old Alvitus'?"

"I do not know, majesty. He never told me. He never told me anything at all except to go and sit and I went and sat."

"The Lord appeared to you?"

"No, He did not. Nor spoke to me either. He just came out of an ambush in my own mind and then He had me. I was minding my own business and avoiding everyone I could. Sheep are quiet company. One day I simply knew that He wanted me to come down here and wait. I can't tell you more than that."

The old man appears to be telling the truth. If he is a charlatan, he is a clever one. God knows, he takes no care to be civil much less to curry favor.

"But after you had this 'revelation', why didn't you consult the bishop, or even the count? Had you no repect for their proper authority?"

"Not much, sire. Anyway, what would I have told them? You know them? Would they have come and sat with me? More likely they would've whipped my back to bloody ribbons. If He had wanted them, the Lord could have sent them the message and left me to my flocks."

Either I have to smile or I have to have him whipped myself, for insolence. The old mule is just as Oro described. The king softened his tone a bit.

"But when my nephew appeared, you took him into your confidence—and your hut."

"Oro was different, my lord. I didn't look for him. He just turned up one day. I didn't pick him. The Lord sent him."

"But he himself doesn't believe that. I've just talked with

him. He's merely a healthy young man who wants very much to be married to a girl with whom he is hopelessly in love. Did you know that?"

"Yes, I've heard that, sire. It doesn't surprise me. Nothing has worked out the way I expected. But I still think that he was sent. Unless I am mistaken, he saved my life more than once. I set myself up to tutor him in the ways of the Lord and instead he became my protector. Was that just a coincidence? Only your authority could have preserved me and this young man turned up bearing it at precisely the right moment. Do you see what I mean?"

"Are you mad, Alvitus?"

"No, your majesty, I am not mad."

"What is in the casket, Alvitus?"

"The bones of the Apostle, Saint James the Great, your majesty."

"How do you know that, Alvitus?"

"The same way I knew all the rest. I just do."

King Alfonso made his decision. He had heard enough. He had seen enough. Now he must be king. It was no longer possible to delay. All the questions had been asked; all the answers had been given.

"I hope that you have learned to sit, that you have learned to like to sit, Alvitus. Because that is what you are going to do for the remainder of your life. You are going to sit before that sarcophagus as long as you live. You are going to be living testimony to what you say that you believe it contains. If you ever leave that vigil, even for a day, I will have the box destroyed and your miserable carcass torn to pieces by my hunting dogs.

"Holy man or not, you are about to become a monk—an abbot even. If need be, I will supply you with monks. You and your disciples will inhabit a monastery here, before the altar dedicated to the Apostle James. You and your fellows will offer veneration to his relics for so long as you shall live—for so long as your successors and theirs shall live. Only the return of Christ Himself will free you from that charge.

"Do I surprise you, old man?"

"I have become accustomed, these past months, to being led where I have not chosen to go, sire."

# Chapter Nineteen

A few of the royal tents had been knocked down and some room thus made just outside the great hall of the comital palace. Into that space now, the whole of the local population, the king's own party, and some visitors from the adjacent districts were slowly gathering. Early arrivals were becoming increasingly restive as the heat of the morning built and the press of bodies became more and more restrictive. For that matter, most of them were ankle deep, or better, in mud.

"Does anybody know what the king is going to say?"

"Let's hope that he's going to tell us that he's taking his damn animals and going home."

"Amen to that! There never was a farmer who didn't like the smell of shit but enough is enough. We need a little fresh air around here more than we need a king."

"What about the animals wearing the swords? If I had a penny for every time one of his soldiers made a grab at my daughter's ass I'd be able to buy a whole new plow team."

"Anybody have a chicken left? We'll have to sleep with them if things get any worse."

The grumbling moderated, for the king had emerged from the great hall and some grooms were carrying out chairs for the royal party. Even at a distance the man commanded. This morning it was not just his height and regal mien. Alfonso had chosen to mark the occasion with a crown-wearing and the diadem caught the light in two dozen great gems that glowed and sparkled in greens, reds, yellows, and milky whites, as though he were wearing a small fire. In addition, over his invariable black, the king wore a splendid robe of purple silk embroidered with leopards and griffins and antelopes in gold and silken threads and itself inset liberally with additional jewels.

On the one side of Alfonso were Count Muño and Bishop Teodemiro carefully dressed to be just less magnificent than their sovereign. The bishop wore his miter and carried the episcopal crook. Only the count wore arms, a long sword in a scabbard of worked bronze whose hilt and guard waxed fantastic with steel vines and lattice. On the other side of the king stood Aurelius and Jimena. Both were clad in tunics of the plainest white but belted in gold. Jimena had flowers of gold worked into her auburn hair as well.

The royal guard had donned its cleanest tunics and their freshly-burnished spears and shields glistened against that dun-colored background. Clearly King Alfonso wished to impress all with the solemnity and the significance of what was about to take place. For greater ease in speaking the king now rose from his seat amidst a sudden hush that fell over the crowd.

"A king," he began, "is never so much a king as when he distributes gifts among his faithful subjects. Now is such a time. The gifts with which I shall reward you today are not small things—coins, or bracelets, or food, or land—although those will have their place here subsequently. My gifts this day are those which will ensure you peace, justice, and prosperity for your own lifetime and that of your children. More, they will promote among you the blessings of God and the guardianship the of His Son, Jesus Christ, and of the apostle of the Lord, Saint James the Great.

"Now the first of these gifts is a wedding that will be celebrated here today."

A murmur of approval ran through the crowd and there were even a few tentative cheers—although they died away quickly. Alfonso turned and extended his hands to Aurelius, drawing him forward slightly.

"Many of you present already know my nephew, Aurelius, for he has lived among you for some months now. Many of you also, I am told, had doubts at first about his identity. There were reasons for that but I declare before you today that he is a legitimate descendant of the royal house of this kingdom, raised and educated in my own palace in Oviedo."

The king now turned and reached his hand to Jimena. In turn, he drew her forward a bit and pressed her hand into that of Aurelius.

"You have no such problems with this young woman. Jimena is the daughter of your count, Muño, and his sole surviving child. She is as well the niece of your bishop, Teodemiro. I am informed also that Bishop Teodemiro has no children of his own."

There was a moment of uncertain silence and then guffaws broke out. Alfonso let them subside of their own and then continued.

"This marriage then will join two young people but it will also join, in the most intimate way, the royal lineage of this kingdom and the comital lineage in this territory. From that union I, your king, expect to reap the benefit of the ever closer loyalty of my subjects in Galicia to my person and to my successors and my descendants. The count, his house, and you yourselves may hope to enjoy, in your own turn, the special warmth of our regard and protection.

Most immediately, this evening you will all celebrate with us the marriage of these two happy young people. As is customary, there will be enough of food and drink for all guests. To show our own special joy in this event we have also decreed a distribution of the royal largesse to celebrate it. All bachelors of either sex here present will receive two pennies, all good married folk will receive five pennies each, and all children a penny."

Now there was spontaneous cheering. King Alfonso allowed it with one of his rare public smiles.

"Our second gift to you on this day has been decided together with your own Count Muño. He has agreed that all of his rights and possessions will pass at his death, hopefully long to be deferred, to his daughter Jimena alone. I, in turn, have decreed that the countship will be bestowed upon my nephew, Aurelius, at that time. In the future then, the oversight of this district will be in the hands of this young couple, representing the best of our two lineages. In the meantime, your count will spare no energies in instructing both of them in the practical matters involved in such supervision. These measures will ensure that the prosperity of Asturias and the well-being of Galicia develop hand in hand and that the safety of both from attack will be guaranteed by the close cooperation that can be expected between them."

When the import of this announcement came home, most eyes in the assemblage sought the faces of Count Muño and his brother, the bishop. Some thought that their smiles appeared forced. "One should not roll dice with a king unless one can afford to lose" was a proverb that most of them knew. Not understanding what reaction, or how much of one, might be expected of them, the people remained awkwardly silent.

"Our final gift to this community will be a church. That is a small thing, a beginning only. God himself has already, in fire and flood, bestowed on you an infinitely precious gift. He has revealed to you the presence on your soil of the bones of his apostle, the great Saint James. For whatever reason, He has chosen this time and our reign to do so. My own nephew Aurelius, your bishop Teodemiro, and your count Muño, as well as the hermit Alvitus, bear testimony to this revelation.

What other response can I make but to see to the construction of a church here, at royal expense, to provide a house for the Apostle and a tabernacle for all of those who will come to visit his shrine? I will as well endow a monastery before the altar of the saint so that Santiago will have the continuous praise and prayer, day after day, that is fitting and due him. And since God Himself has selected the man, what else can I do except to install the hermit, Alvitus, as the first abbot of this monastery? Your own Bishop Teodemiro agrees that all these actions are proper and due.

Our generation, yours and mine, has seen a great light from the heavens. The Lord has chosen to reveal his saint to us. We are amazed. We had no warning. We do not understand. The ways of the Lord are mysterious.

It may be that He is not finished here. At the very end of the earth He has chosen to raise up a sign. What are we to make of this? Can we think otherwise than that He has taken the Christian people of Hispania under His protection? Can we think any less than that? Should we not understand that the long time of trial and suffering under the yoke of the Africans approaches its end? And if He has made us so wonderful a gift, has He not also imposed upon us the duty of His service? And who but the crown should be His first servant?

The world will come to be amazed at the rebirth of this land under the protection of the Apostle James. Through all the lands that serve the Lord, people will wonder at what He has wrought and perhaps will come to worship as well in this, the place of our deliverance."

* * *

The voice of King Alfonso II has died away. The voices of the bards who sang his praise have perished. The little church that he had raised over the sarcophagus of marble has vanished. But in the place of that church one yet larger grew, only itself still later to yield to a Romanesque cathedral of heroic proportions. And that cathedral, in turn, has been clothed and cloaked over the centuries in the gold-hued stone of addition after addition whose spires glisten yet in the sunlight of afternoons.

The rule of Galicia and Santiago de Compostela has passed to the lawyers, the men of the south, who nevertheless still solemnly observe the Año Santo, the holy year, whenever the feast of Saint James the Great on July 25 happens to fall upon a Sunday.

For five hundred years the great pilgrim hospital of Ferdinand and Isabella, raised in gratitude to the Apostle for the final victory over Muslim power in the peninsula in 1492, has sat next to the church of Santiago. For the pilgrims did come. By tens, then by hundreds, by thousands, and by tens of thousands they came—and come still. The earth groans with the weight of the pilgrims and the stones sink under their burden.